Contributions to Economics

The series *Contributions to Economics* provides an outlet for innovative research in all areas of economics. Books published in the series are primarily monographs and multiple author works that present new research results on a clearly defined topic, but contributed volumes and conference proceedings are also considered. All books are published in print and ebook and disseminated and promoted globally. The series and the volumes published in it are indexed by Scopus and ISI (selected volumes).

Stefan Walzer
Editor

Digital Healthcare in Germany

Market Access for Innovations

Springer

Editor
Stefan Walzer
MArS Market Access & Pricing Strategy
GmbH
Weil am Rhein, Germany

State University Baden-Wuerttemberg
Lörrach, Germany

RWU – Ravensburg-Weingarten
University of Applied Sciences
Weingarten, Germany

ISSN 1431-1933 ISSN 2197-7178 (electronic)
Contributions to Economics
ISBN 978-3-030-94024-9 ISBN 978-3-030-94025-6 (eBook)
https://doi.org/10.1007/978-3-030-94025-6

This Springer imprint is published by the registered company Springer Nature Switzerland AG
The registered company address is: Gewerbestrasse 11, 6330 Cham, Switzerland

Contents

Introduction

Stefan Walzer

The term digital healthcare encompasses a wide range of innovative fields that extends far beyond regional and national borders. Spurred on by striving to improve the individual's state of health, research is being performed to implement ideas based on modern technologies, to develop optimization potentials and to make these usable for the benefit of all those involved (and beyond).

Against the backdrop of an aging society, the shortage of skilled workers and in general scarce resources for health services, there is a need for active action in almost all conceivable areas to maintain and improve the future quality of healthcare for people affected. In addition to other benefits, digitalization in the healthcare system offers people from structurally weak and remote regions, and those who do not have sufficient mobility, the potential for equitable and targeted healthcare.

From an economic perspective, innovations can be at the level of new products, optimized processes and organizational improvements (Chapter "Innovation, Incentives, and Information Technology in the Healthcare Industry"). Theoretically, information technology (IT) has the potential to have a positive impact on innovations in all these areas. Which innovations will ultimately prevail, however, depends, in addition to financial influencing factors, in particular on the interests of the institutions involved and groups of people involved or affected.

The path from the idea to actually implemented innovation is long and requires, in addition to the commitment of all actors involved, in particular an adequate legal foundation (Chapter "Digital Health Applications: DiGAs: Pathway to Reimbursement"). In the outpatient setting, this foundation has been implemented as part of the

S. Walzer (✉)
MArS Market Access & Pricing Strategy GmbH, Weil am Rhein, Germany

State University Baden-Wuerttemberg, Lörrach, Germany

RWU – Ravensburg-Weingarten University of Applied Sciences, Weingarten, Germany
e-mail: Stefan.walzer@marketaccess-pricingstrategy.de

S. Walzer (ed.), *Digital Healthcare in Germany*, Contributions to Economics,
https://doi.org/10.1007/978-3-030-94025-6_1

Digital Healthcare Act (DVG) in Germany to pave the market's way towards these new approaches as part of a "fast-track market access process".

Despite the increasing number of initiatives, it cannot be overlooked that Germany more or less missed the go-ahead for digitization in the healthcare system until 2020 (Chapter "Inpatient Market Access for Digital Health"). This was expressed by a digital infrastructure in the extensive hospital landscape that could be classified as inadequate, especially in comparison to other countries. The key word here is funding. While short-term hospital funding at the federal macro level usually failed due to bureaucratic hurdles and insufficient resources being made available at the meso level of federal states, optimization with regard to digital health remained at the micro level; and therefore primarily at hospitals themselves. Against the backdrop of competitiveness and adequate patient care, there was an urgent need for action in the digital health field in Germany.

In future, it is to be expected that, especially in nursing, an increasing number of tasks, with regard to inpatient and outpatient care, will be taken over by innovations from the fields of robotics and digitization (Chapter "Digitalization of Nursing to Overcome Staffing Shortages? Categorization and Market Access of Digital Applications"). Possible uses here are varied and range from interactive offers to technical aids and documentation options. However, despite all the euphoria and all the possibilities in the context of digital health, it must also be recognized that active support in the area of standard care services is still a long way off.

The profitability of a digital health application is defined by its price, which must be carefully planned in advance by the respective manufacturer. The price must be either cost-oriented, value-added or strategically determined (Chapter "Reimbursement and Pricing").

But how does Germany measure up against other countries potentially at the forefront of digital healthcare, namely Japan and the United States of America? While Australia, China and the USA are considered to be pioneers in the field of telemedicine, the example of Japan makes it clear that for further growth, the technological readiness of both the elderly and geriatricians are especially relevant (Chapter "Telemedicine in Japan: Challenges and Opportunities"). In addition, although Japan is one of the few countries in which digital health apps are reimbursed by health insurance companies as the market access pathway is the same as for drugs and medical devices. Furthermore, the reimbursement rates for telemedical applications are relatively low compared to conventional face-to-face consultations with physicians. While an increased demand for telemedicine services was observed during the COVID-19 pandemic, face-to-face interactions with physicians are still the norm.

In the USA, several companies are developing digital health applications for patients, nurses and providers that have the potential to optimize processes while reducing costs (Chapter "Barriers and Opportunities for Digital Therapeutics in the United States"). The framework for this is a legal basis that focuses on value creation in the provision of services and is particularly useful in the case of chronic diseases. While there is a benefit, a significant impact on patient care has not yet been demonstrated. To optimize the situation, an integrative approach is sought, in which the acceptance of useful technologies is to be promoted by supporting the cooperation of the actors involved. An essential point for the lack of acceptance is due to uncertainty regarding the costs, effectiveness and efficiency of health applications. In addition to obtaining regulatory approval, ensuring reimbursement is a central issue in the US. In any case, there are different pathways available to collect reimbursement such as the patient's out-of-pocket expenses, employer reimbursement and hospital funding.

Digital Healthcare in Germany: An Overview

Stefan Walzer

Digitalization is also referred to as the "industrial revolution" of the twenty-first century. In many industries, it has been introduced in routine processes, although it is not yet "common practice" in the healthcare sector. Legal and technical prerequisites exist, but what exactly is the current state of digital possibilities in the healthcare sector in Germany?

The term digitalization can be defined in many ways. On the one hand, the term stands for the digital conversion and representation of information. On the other, digitalization is also often associated with the process of digital modification. It is also credited with the major benefit of improving the speed of communication channels (Cf. Deckert 2019, p. 7 f). Digitalization is spreading across various sectors and is also increasingly affecting the provision of healthcare. Due to the diverse interests of various players, this is proving to be a complex process. Challenges include the digitalization of documents and the processing of large volumes of data. The opportunities presented by the expanding process of digitalization can be seen in the context of innovations and new technologies. Important considerations here are adaptations to legal framework conditions, but also reforms. The expansion of digitalization also creates the possibility of designing new healthcare services, for which active co-design by the patient is a fundamental criterion (Cf. Da Cruz et al. 2017, p. V f).

If we now consider the concept of digitalization in healthcare, we can say that digital healthcare encompasses various areas. On the one hand, it creates new diagnostic and treatment options, such as personalized medicine, and on the other,

S. Walzer (✉)
MArS Market Access & Pricing Strategy GmbH, Weil am Rhein, Germany

State University Baden-Wuerttemberg, Lörrach, Germany

RWU – Ravensburg-Weingarten University of Applied Sciences, Weingarten, Germany
e-mail: Stefan.walzer@marketaccess-pricingstrategy.de

S. Walzer (ed.), *Digital Healthcare in Germany*, Contributions to Economics,
https://doi.org/10.1007/978-3-030-94025-6_2

Table 1 Areas of digital health and explanations

Digital health area	Explanation
Artificial intelligence (AI)	AI learns from digital health data and can recognize patterns. This can help doctors in diagnostics and decision-making
Big data	As a result of the digitalization of healthcare, the amount of data is rapidly growing. This data can be used to detect the risk of diseases earlier. Personalized healthcare is also based on big data
Telemedicine	Telemedicine uses modern communication solutions for the purposes of remote monitoring, diagnostics, and therapy. It facilitates care in rural areas (for example in the application of video consultations)
E-health	This term covers all applications that use new information and communication technologies in the provision of medical care, for example the electronic health card
Robotics	Robot-assisted procedures can be used in the operating room and in nursing care; they are mainly used as assistance systems

Source: author's own representation based on PricewaterhouseCoopers GmbH (n.d.)

it enables easier communication among the individual players in the healthcare system. In addition, individual patients can take greater control of their health, for example through apps. Digitalization in the healthcare sector creates the opportunity to counteract the shortage of skilled workers and significantly relieve the burden on doctors and nurses in areas such as administrative activities and documentation, diagnostics, and everyday practical activities (Cf. PricewaterhouseCoopers GmbH n.d.). The different areas of digital health are presented in Table 1.

Due to demographic changes in society, the number of elderly and people suffering from chronic diseases and multimorbidity is growing. This is increasingly becoming a challenge in the healthcare sector, because an aging society makes greater use of medical services. Other existing challenges are the shortage of skilled workers in the nursing and medical professions and underuse of medical services in structurally weaker regions.

However, because the German healthcare system is characterized by an innovation-inhibiting structure and financial imbalance, the digital optimization of operational processes and care innovations is consequently also made more difficult. This is also shown by the DIGITAL Economy Index of the German Federal Ministry for Economic Affairs and Energy (BMWi), which measures sector-specific progress in digital transformation. Here, the German healthcare sector performed comparatively poorly in 2018, scoring 37 out of 100 points (Cf. Pfannstiel et al. 2020, p. 254). The Healthcare Information and Management Systems Society (HIMMS) also came to similar conclusions. In its Analytics Electronic Medical Record Adoption Model (EMRAM), which measures the digitalization of institutions on a scale from zero (no digitalization) to seven (paperless hospital), German hospitals scored only 2.3 in 2017. They are thus significantly below average in terms of digitalization compared with other countries (e.g. Denmark 5.4, Turkey 3.8) and the European average (3.6) (Cf. Klauber et al. 2019, p. 17 ff).

Up to now, digital isolated solutions have prevailed in the German health care system, preventing interdepartmental networking. This is set to change with the expansion of the telematics infrastructure. At the end of 2018, a wake-up call went through Germany when the Bertelsmann Foundation's highly regarded Digital Health Index provided evidence of how far Germany lags behind other countries in terms of digitalisation: It ranked 16th out of 17 countries compared, with only Poland scoring lower. Since then, however, a lot has happened in the digitisation of the German healthcare system. The Federal Ministry of Health, health innovation hub, gematik, the National Association of Statutory Health Insurance Physicians (Kassenärztliche Bundesvereinigung) and leading health insurance funds have initiated, driven forward and implemented many reform projects in recent years. Since the end of 2017, doctors' and dentists' surgeries have been successively equipped with the necessary technology to guarantee a fast and secure exchange of relevant patient data. The introduction of the "app on prescription" and the associated remuneration of digital health applications (DiGA) will in all likelihood stimulate patient demand for electronic health aids. McKinsey's eHealth App Barometer, which measures app usage based on download figures, shows how dynamically the market for health apps is developing in Germany: At the first peak of the Covid-19 crisis in the first quarter of 2020, health apps and services came to almost two million downloads—a doubling compared to the same period last year.

At first glance, the connection of doctors to the telematics infrastructure seems to be progressing rapidly: According to expert estimates, 85% of all physicians in private practice and 98% of all dentists now have the technical prerequisites. However, the scope of use still leaves much to be desired—the practices currently only transmit patient master data. A broader exchange of information would require the introduction of comprehensive standards across the board, but these have only existed in part so far.

Nevertheless, digitalization is becoming increasingly important in healthcare. This applies in particular to the exchange of data and information among all those involved in a patient's treatment. Communication between doctor and patient is also being transformed by digitalization. For this reason, the term telemedicine is closely linked to digital healthcare. This may refer, for example, to video consultations, which are becoming increasingly common. However, outpatient digital care includes other methods of supporting medical care. For example, the Digital Care Act (DVG), which came into effect on December 19, 2019, explicitly includes the use of health apps, among other things. The term ambulatory digital care thus describes all digital measures that support ambulatory care.

Digital expansion in the healthcare sector is accompanied by high costs and is therefore associated with increasing cost pressure. At the same time, however, it represents an opportunity to create new business models (Cf. Dachtler et al. 2017, p. 241 f). New approaches and solutions must be established above all for immobile and high-risk patients and in rural areas, where there is a lack of (specialist) medical care. The opportunity for better healthcare lies primarily in digital care structures and digitalization. A study conducted by the Bertelsmann Foundation in 2018 analyzed how actively the healthcare policies of different countries are acting on digitalization. Of the 17 countries surveyed, Germany came in 16th place. An international comparison therefore shows that German healthcare policy has a lot of catching up to do in terms of expanding digitalization.

Furthermore, the problem of the increasing shortage of nursing specialists is already widely known in Germany. As of August 30, 2020, the number of people in need of care was 3,414,378 (Cf. Gesundheitsberichterstattung des Bundes 2020), and this number will continue to rise in the future. According to forecasts by the German Federal Statistical Office (Destatis), up to five million people will be in need of care in 2025. At the same time, there are fewer and fewer caregivers to look after such people. In 2025, there is expected to be a shortfall of around 500,000 care professionals (Cf. Heeser 2020, p. 10). At the same time, increasing digitalization is making itself felt in all areas. Healthcare players—doctors, clinics, practices, and patients—are already having to deal with many digital innovations (Cf. Deutsche Gesellschaft für Orthopädie und Unfallchirurgie n.d.). These digital innovations, as well as assistive technologies, offer great potential benefits for the healthcare sector (Cf. Elmer 2017, p. 23). For example, the shortage of skilled workers described above could be countered by using new solutions that relieve staff of time, physical, and informational burdens. In addition, modern nursing aids can not only support staff but also increase the attractiveness of the nursing profession (Cf. Graf 2019, p. 20).

The latest point at which the "app on prescription" for patients was introduced into healthcare was when the DVG came into force, thus laying an important foundation stone for advancing digital healthcare in Germany. As a result, around 73 million people insured under the statutory health insurance scheme are entitled to the provision of digital health apps. These can be prescribed by doctors and psychotherapists, for example, and are then reimbursed by the health insurer of the patient.

For this reason, German policymakers are striving to expand the digitalization of the healthcare system by, among other things, providing and expanding a secure infrastructure for digital care through the Gesellschaft für Telematik (Society for Telematics), and by strengthening and promoting digital care structures, for example through new legislation. As a result of the DVG, for example, the areas of "electronic patient records," "health apps," and "video consultations" in particular have been strengthened and integrated into everyday care. Digital healthcare structures, which have so far been underutilized in Germany, are therefore currently becoming increasingly important in nationwide healthcare provision.

The following provides an insight into some lighthouse projects in digital care. Because medical care in Germany is divided into outpatient and inpatient care, the following examples are divided accordingly. Outpatient care includes all treatment services that are provided without an overnight stay in a clinical facility. Inpatient care involves staying in a hospital for medical treatment and is provided if the treatment goal cannot be achieved on an outpatient basis.

1 Outpatient Care

Telemedicine is already being used, predominantly in funded pilot projects and individual cases. Legal framework conditions have already been created for this in the DVG. The application areas of telemedicine can support both the physician and non-physician nursing and medical staff in their activities. In addition to the DiGA (digital health applications) process (see chapter "Inpatient Market Access for Digital Health"), there are other options in the outpatient care sector that can be used to introduce digital care solutions, especially if they are not a DiGA, into the German healthcare market.

1.1 The Innovation Fund (IF)

The IF was adopted in 2015 with the Act to Strengthen Care in Statutory Health Insurance (GKV, Versorgungsstärkungsgesetz) and came into force in 2016. The overarching goal of the IF is to further develop the quality of care provided by the statutory health insurance (SHI) system. To achieve this goal, the IF's funding is divided into two areas: forms of care and care research. On the one hand, the funding is intended to support new forms of care in SHI that go beyond standard SHI care and have the potential to be included in care on a permanent basis. On the other hand, financial support is to be given to new research projects aimed at gaining knowledge to improve existing care (Cf. Hecken 2017, p. 462). The funds for the IF come from the liquidity reserve of the Health Fund and the statutory health insurance funds and, accordingly, indirectly from the contributors to SHI (Cf. Pollandt 2017, p. 466 f). From 2016 until 2019 inclusive, 300 million euros was made available annually, 80% of which was for new forms of care and 20% for health services research (Cf. Gemeinsamer Bundesausschuss Innovationsausschuss 2020, p. 1 ff). Because only a few IF projects have been completed so far, it is not yet possible to conclude the extent to which the IF project results will ultimately find their way into standard care.

The decision-making body for the IF's funding decisions is the Innovation Committee (IA, Innovationsausschuss). This is composed of three representatives of the GKV Spitzenverband (National Association of Statutory Health Insurance Funds); one representative each of the Kassenärztliche Bundesvereinigung (National Association of Statutory Health Insurance Physicians), the Kassenzahnärztliche Bundesvereinigung (National Association of Statutory Health Insurance Dentists), and the Deutsche Krankenhausgesellschaft (German Hospital Federation); the impartial chairman of the Federal Joint Committee (G-BA); two representatives of the Federal Ministry of Health; and one representative of the Federal Ministry of Education and Research. In addition, two patient representatives sit on the IA, but they have no voting rights, only the right to submit proposals and to participate in consultations. The IA determines funding priorities and criteria for the allocation of funding from the IF. On this basis, applications for funding can be submitted, and the

IA decides whether the project in question should be funded. A majority of seven votes is required to pass decisions by the IA.

One example of digital care that was supported by the IF and is now to be transferred to standard care is the Telenotarzt (remote emergency doctor service) in Bavaria. The goal of the Telenotarzt Bavaria project was to optimize emergency care in a rural region. Here, the emergency ("Telenot") physician supports the rescue service from a distance during call-outs. The patient's vital signs are measured on site, transmitted from the ambulance to the emergency physician, and immediately analyzed by him or her for diagnosis and initial treatment. This means that the patient's treatment can begin sooner. Because emergency medical services are regulated by state laws, the findings obtained are forwarded to the health ministries of the federal states. These ministries will decide whether the Telenotarzt concept can be usefully established in their federal state and whether existing state laws governing rescue services may have to be reformed for this purpose. The project was approved for transfer to standard care by the Joint Federal Committee on December 18, 2020.

1.2 Selective Contracts

Like collective contracts, selective contracts are independent forms of contract in the healthcare system. However, whereas collective contracts in the outpatient sector are concluded between the associations of health insurers and the associations of SHI-accredited physicians, selective contracts are concluded directly among individual service providers (physician, hospital, pharmaceutical company, etc.) and one or more health insurers. Health insurance funds can conclude selective contracts in the following circumstances:

- model projects (§§ 63 ff. SGB V [German Social Code, Book 5])
- the Disease Management Program (§§ 137 f. SGB V)
- special care (§ 140a SGB V) such as integrated care.

As a result, insured persons have access to treatment options to which they would not be entitled without a selective contract. Thus, contracting between health insurers and service providers promotes innovation in the healthcare system and strengthens competition among health insurers (Cf. Müller 2015).

The following examines the selective contract "Telemedicine Heart," which was concluded between the health insurance fund Techniker Krankenkasse and the Robert Bosch Hospital in Stuttgart and the company Phillips. Within the framework of a telemedical program, insured persons diagnosed with heart failure are individually monitored and looked after for 1 year. This offer is not considered a substitute for personal doctor–patient contact, but as a useful supplement to it. Since July 2017, 333 participants have completed the program, while 281 participants are still in ongoing care.

The patient uses a tablet to carry out daily monitoring of his or her health values and transmits them to the telemedicine team at Robert Bosch Hospital. There, the data is monitored by specialists who are also available as contact persons and who contact the insured person in case of abnormalities. The attending physician can obtain information about the patient's state of health from the Robert Bosch Hospital at any time and optimize the therapy accordingly. In addition, the tablet regularly offers training videos that are adapted to the patient's particular health situation. This provides additional information and support for outpatient treatment.

An evaluation of the selective contract was planned for the end of 2020. This means that there will be a performance audit in which the costs and benefits are analyzed by the health insurer. The Joint Federal Committee also examines the benefit provided by this care by means of a method evaluation. If the cost–benefit assessment is positive, this form of treatment can be included in the standard care provided by the health insurance funds.

Another selectively contracted digital care option is the "TeleArzt-Rucksack" (tele-doctor backpack). The project is described as a supportive, telemedical, and general practitioner (GP) delegation model. In the future, the project is expected to cross sector boundaries between care facilities and outpatient home-based care, leading to an improvement in care. The provision of competent telemedical care as a combination of documentation aids, video technology, and measuring devices creates a care solution that represents a new form of treatment.

The TeleArzt-Rucksack is equipped with six sensors:

- telemedicine pulse oximeter
- telemedicine spirometer
- telemedicine blood-pressure monitor
- telemedicine blood-glucose meter
- telemedical vitaphone 3-channel electrocardiogram
- telemedicine personal scale.

The equipment in the TeleArzt-Rucksack enables the medical assistant (Mfa)—who must undergo additional training—to measure the patient's values directly at home and transfer them to the doctor's systems using a tablet. If necessary, it is also possible to use a tablet included in the rucksack to conduct video consultations with the primary care physician, for example to discuss medication or fill out questionnaires. The aim of the project is to increase capacity by improving efficiency and quality in outpatient primary care.

The TeleArzt-Rucksack is already in use in 12 of 19 Kassenärztliche Vereinigung (KV, Association of Statutory Health Insurance Physicians) districts. Thuringia was the first federal state to make the care model available statewide. The first telemedicine area contract in Germany was signed in April 2018 between the general local health insurance fund AOK PLUS and KV Thuringia. Techniker Krankenkasse in Thuringia is also the first major substitute health insurer to honor the TeleArzt. In Lower Saxony, the TeleArzt has been used in the city of Gifhorn since mid-2019. The pilot phase of the project was completed in November 2018 and received a positive evaluation from GPs, the Lower Saxony KV, politicians, and the AOK. The contribution made by the TeleArzt-Rucksack convinced the Lower Saxony AOK to include the project in their service catalog. The parties mentioned above decided to continue and expand the project in Lower Saxony. Likewise, the state government of Lower Saxony sought an extension to 2021 if the project continues to prove its worth. The Lower Saxony health regions will provide financing in the region of 80,000 euros until the end of 2020. It is not only family doctors who benefit from using the TeleArzt-Rucksack. The MfA, who provides home visits instead of the doctor, also profits from this project. It facilitates the documentation of service providers, because the transmission takes place automatically. The MfA can also take on additional tasks, such as wound documentation, and, in the event of abnormalities, can be put in touch via teleconsultation with the doctor, who will assess the clinical picture (Cf. Vitagroup AG 2020a).

The state government in Thuringia decided on a funding program and has been supporting physicians in the procurement of TeleArzt rucksacks since April 1, 2019. The TeleArzt is also being used by the state government in Schleswig-Holstein to support telemedical care there (Cf. Vitagroup AG 2020b).

2 Inpatient Care

In general, hospital services are differentiated according to Section 39 of the German Social Code, Book V (SGB V) into full and partial inpatient services, pre- and post-inpatient services, and outpatient operations. The remuneration of elective services is based on a separate contractual agreement between the hospital and the patient (Cf. GKV Spitzenverband 2019). The DRG (Diagnosis-Related Groups) system according to Section 17b of the German Hospital Financing Act (KHG, Krankenhausfinanzierungsgesetz) forms the basis for the financing of full and partial inpatient services. Further legal regulations for individual variants of remuneration can also be found in the Hospital Remuneration Act (KHEntgG) and in the flat rate per case agreement of the self-governing partners (Cf. Bundesministerium für Gesundheit 2020). The DRG system is a patient classification system and forms the core of the payment system for inpatient services.

In hospitals, the principle of "permission with prohibition" applies, i.e. in principle, examination and treatment methods (NUB) can be used as long as they have not been excluded by the G-BA according to § 137c SGB.

The financing of investments in recent years has declined, resulting in an investment backlog of at least 30 billion euros. An investment gap of almost four million euros is created each year. As a result, urgent investments—for example, in buildings, medical technology, and digitalization—cannot be made. Due to the withdrawal of funding by the federal states, hospitals often have to finance the investments themselves. This is done with the help of loans or via internal financing, in which hospitals increase revenues for given operating costs or try to save on personnel and material costs for given revenues.

Various regulatory options are available to fund digital health solutions in the inpatient setting, which are introduced in detail in chapter "Inpatient Market Access for Digital Health". These regulations include the Hospital Futures Act for the digitalization of hospitals, which is an investment program designed to counteract the investment backlog. Additionally, under Section 68a of Book V of the SGB, health insurance funds have been given the opportunity to participate directly in the promotion of digital innovations. Under the Act, they can either:

- participate in a development in cooperation with manufacturers of medical devices, companies from the field of information technology, research institutions, and service providers and communities of service providers, or
- acquire shares in the investment fund.

Thus, health insurers have been given the opportunity to promote and finance new innovations in collaboration with hospitals.

Examples of advancing digital care in inpatient facilities can be found in many processes, including:

- voice recognition systems that patients can use to call a nurse or lower blinds in their rooms
- inpatient wristbands with an embedded chip or a printed code.

In the latter example, if a mobile patient has an appointment for an electroencephalogram (EEG), he or she can "check in" at a terminal using his or her wristband. This automatically notifies the EEG department staff that the patient is in the waiting area. The EEG findings, documents, and doctor's letters are stored digitally for each new patient and are thus available to all parties involved at any time or place (electronic patient file).[9]

According to studies, 5–10% of all hospital patients receive the wrong medication during their stay. The electronic patient record (ePA) and associated systems are therefore intended to make hospital treatment safer for patients. Closed Loop Medication Management (CLMM) refers to a closed loop in which all steps of the medication prescription process are digitized (Cf. Maier 2020, p. 19). The Hamburg-Eppendorf University Medical Center (UKE) is considered a pioneer for introducing this particular medication process. The UKE is one of the most modern university hospitals in Europe and in 2011 was the first European hospital to receive the highest possible score (7.0) in EMRAM for having introduced a completely digital patient record. The project to introduce the ePA also included the conversion of drug supply from traditional ward cabinet logistics to a patient-oriented unit-dose procedure, which is a part of the CLMM. The unit-dose process makes solid drugs available for oral use in individual packages. For this purpose, the previously handwritten medication plans were replaced by digital plans, and a closed medication process, the so-called closed loop process, was established.

Doctors and scientists at Freiburg University Hospital (UKF) have been researching for years how intelligent programs can support the work performed in clinics. One example of their research can be found in the evaluation of microscope images, which are crucial for many diagnoses. In the Department of Ophthalmology at the UKF, microscopic images of the endothelial layer, a wafer-thin layer of cells in the eye, must be viewed regularly. The endothelial cells keep the cornea in the eye transparent by continuously pumping water out of the cornea. However, when the cells die, the cornea becomes cloudy. For this reason, the endothelial cells must be counted regularly to determine the right time for treatment. For a long time, physicians counted the cells by hand, which was both time-consuming and prone to error. The evaluation is now done by a self-learning piece of software, which was developed by the team at the eye clinic. The software has been trained on hundreds of hand-counted images and can now provide an evaluation of the microscopic images within a few seconds. This frees up physicians' time for other activities and reduces the error rate tremendously. In addition, the software can be used in future studies to examine significantly more images than before, which will make these studies more precise (Cf. Universitätsklinikum Freiburg 2019, p. 18).

Other examples of the advancing digitalization at the UKF can be found in the areas of training and surgery planning. In the urology outpatient clinic, students practice catheter placement on a model during their internship. Augmented reality (AR) glasses support the students' learning. The AR glasses contain a tiny camera that detects what is in the user's field of vision. Helpful tips and information on the next step of catheter placement are then displayed on the semi-transparent lens. Virtual reality is also used in surgery planning. Surgeons can, for example, use a 3D model to practice hand movements before operating on the brain (Cf. Universitätsklinikum Freiburg 2019, p. 27) or "play through how best to work their way between blood vessels and sensitive structures to a tumor" (Universitätsklinikum Freiburg 2019, p. 28). Practicing can make even the most difficult operations safer for the patient (Cf. Universitätsklinikum Freiburg 2019, p. 28).

Financing of digital medicine in the inpatient sector can be realized within the framework of dual hospital financing, provided that the hospital is included in the hospital plan of the state. Further details are included in chapter "Inpatient Market Access for Digital Health".

The financing of digital care in nursing homes requires the involvement of the nursing care insurance funds, e.g. for the purchase of digital aids. The fact that digital aids are financed via individual insurance benefits—i.e. the nursing home can use the devices for only one resident—is seen as an obstacle to the spread of technical aids. To date, the following options exist for refinancing digital care:

- funding under the Nursing Staff Strengthening Act (PpSG, Pflegepersonal-Stärkungsgesetz)
- entitlement within the framework of the catalog of aids
- telecare/telemedicine reimbursement
- robotics reimbursement.

In accordance with Section 82 of the SGB, Book XI, care facilities receive a so-called care allowance, which is used to remunerate general care services as well as a fee for room and board. The care allowance is also known as the care rate. The care allowance is paid by the person in need of care or their cost bearer, while the fee for room and board must be paid by the person in need of care themselves. The care-rate amount is determined by the care-rate agreement concluded between the facility operator and the cost bearers. Performance-related nursing rates are to be assessed according to uniform principles for all residents of the home. "Performance-related" means that the nursing rates are adjusted according to the respective degree of nursing care (Cf. §82 and 84 SGB XI). In addition, the nursing facility is allowed to charge separately for capital expenditures required for operations or for rent, leases, etc (Cf. Braeske et al. 2019, p. 36 f). The so-called training levy is intended to equalize the costs of training between facilities that train a lot and those that train less. In 2020, the training levy in each full inpatient care facility was €1.25/day (Cf. KVJS (2020, n.d.).

Case conferences in nursing can now also take place via video. Previously, they could already be conducted with nursing homes if a cooperation agreement existed for the insured person (Cf. Kassenärztliche Bundesvereinigung 2020). They can be billed by the attending physician or psychotherapist three times per treatment case in accordance with the standardized assessment scale (EBM). Only the physician or psychotherapist who initiated the video case conference receives a technology surcharge.

To acquire the systems and necessary technical equipment for conducting video case conferences, the care facility can take advantage of funding under the Nursing Staff Strengthening Act. In 2018, the Nursing Employers' Association called for telecare to be included in the standard provision of nursing care and recommended that the legislature include existing telecare projects in the SHI benefits catalog.

The new introduction of Digital Care Applications (DiPA), which are to be financed by the Social Care Insurance, is also planned. The Federal Institute for Drugs and Medical Devices (BfArM) will be given responsibility for a procedure to check the reimbursability of DiPA; it is also to set up a DiPA directory as a web portal. The procedure will be set up on two tracks, in alignment with the DiGA procedure, in order to allow both permanent and provisional inclusion of a DiPA in the directory."

References

Braeske, G. et al. (2019): Einsatz von robotischen Systemen in der Pflege in Japan mit Blick auf den steigenden Fachkräftebedarf, Berlin, URL: https://www.bmwi.de/Redaktion/DE/Publikationen/Studien/einsatz-von-robotischen-systemen-pflege-japan_pdf?_blob=publicationFile&v=4, 23.08.2020.

Bundesministerium für Gesundheit. (2020): Krankenhausfinanzierung, URL: https://www.bundesgesundheitsmi-nisterium.de/krankenhausfinanzierung.html, 09.09.2020.

Da Cruz, P., Mehlich, H., Pfannstiehl, M. (2017) (Ed.): Digitale Transformation von Dienstleistungen im Gesundheitswesen II, Impulse für das Management, Wiesbaden: Springer.

Dachtler, M., Edinger, D., Huber, G. (2017): Digitalisierung in der Pharmaindustrie, in: Da Cruz, P., Mehlich, H., Pfannstiehl, M. (Ed.): Digitale Transformation von Dienstleistungen im Gesundheitswesen II, Impulse für das Management, Wiesbaden: Springer.

Deckert, R. (2019): Digitalisierung und Industrie 4.0, technologischer Wandel und individuelle Weiterentwicklung, Wiesbaden: Springer.
Deutsche Gesellschaft für Orthopädie und Unfallchirurgie. (n.d.): AG Digitalisierung, URL: https://dgou.de/gremien/arbeitsgemeinschaften/digitalisierung/, 30.08.2020.
Elmer, Arno. (2017): Die Digitalisierung des Gesundheitswesens, in: Jg. 17, Heft 3 (Ed.: Wissenschaftliches Institut der AOK), p. 23–30.
Gemeinsamer Bundesausschuss Innovationsausschuss. (2020): Der Innovationsfonds: Stand der Dinge.
Gesundheitsberichterstattung des Bundes. (2020): Pflegebedürftige (Anzahl und Quote), URL: http://www.gbebund.de/oowa921install/servlet/oowa/aw92/dboowasys921.xwdevkit/xwd_init?gbe.isgbetol/xs_start_neu/&p_aid=i&p_aid=3331776&nummer=510&p_sprache=D&p_indsp=-&p_aid=80033711, 30.08.2020.
GKV-Spitzenverband. (2019): Fokus: Krankenhausfinanzierung, URL: https://www.gkv-spitzenver-band.de/gkv_spitzenverband/presse/fokus/krankenhausfinan-zierung/thema_krankenhausfinanzierung.jsp, 17.09.2020
Graf, B. (2019): Neue Servicerobotik-Lösungen für die stationäre Pflege, in: PFLEGE Zeitschrift: 1-2.2019 / 72, p. 20-23.
Hecken, J. (2017): Innovationsfonds, in: Forum, 32. Jg., Nr. 6, p. 462 - 465.
Heeser, A. (2020): Schöne digitale Welt, in: PFLEGE Zeitschrift: 9.2020 / 73, p. 10-12.
Kassenärztliche Bundesvereinigung. (2020): Videosprechstunde, URL: https://www.kbv.de/html/videosprechstunde.php, 28.08.2020.
Klauber, J. et al. (2019): Krankenhaus-Report 2019, Das digitale Krankenhaus, Berlin.
KVJS. (2020): Ergebnisse aus dem Erhebungsverfahren Altenpflegeausbildungsumlage 2020, URL: https://www.kvjs.de/fileadmin/dateien/soziales/aav/2020-ergebnisse-aav.pdf, 01.09.2020.
KVJS. (n.d.): Vertragsrecht und Vergütungen, URL: https://www.kvjs.delsozialeslvertragsrecht-und-verguetungen/altenpflege-ausbildungsumlage/, 01.09.2020.
Maier, J. (2020): Der digitale Kreis, in: CNE.magazin, Ausgabe 04/2020, Stuttgart.
Müller, E. (2015): Impulse im Versorgungswettbewerb, URL: https://www.vdek.com/magazin/ausgaben/2015-0102/titel-versorgungswettbewerb.html, 21.08.2020.
Pfannstiel, M., Kassel, K., Rasche, C. (2020): Innovationen und Innovationsmanagement im Gesundheitswesen, Technologien, Produkte und Dienstleistungen voranbringen, Wiesbaden: Springer.
Pollandt, A. (2017): Förderung von Innovationen in der gesetzlichen Krankenversicherung. In: Forum 32 (6), p. 466 - 469.
PricewaterhouseCoopers GmbH. (n.d.): Digitalisierung im Gesundheitswesen, URL: https://www.pwc.de/de/gesundheitswesen-undpharma/digitalisierung-im-gesundheitswesen.html, 30.08.2020.
Universitätsklinikum Freiburg. (2019): Das Magazin - Digitale Medizin, Ausgabe 03/2019, URL: https://www.uniklinik-freiburg.de/fileadmin/mediapool/06_presse/pdfs-publikationenldasma-gazin/2019/UKF_DasMagazin_3_2019.pdf, 13.08.2020.
Vitagroup AG. (2020a): TelePflege verbindet hausärztliche Versorgung und Pflege, URL: https://www.vitagroup.ag/de_DE/News-Insights/Projekt-Gifhorn, 04.09.2020.
Vitagroup AG. (2020b): TeleArzt: bessere und effizientere medizinische Versorgung, URL: https://www.vitagroup.ag/de_DE/News-Insights/TeleArzt-bessere-effizientere-medizinische-Versorgung, 04.09.2020.

Innovation, Incentives, and Information Technology in the Healthcare Industry

Peter Zweifel

1 Product, Process, and Organizational Innovation and a Puzzle Explained

Most writers on the subject distinguish between product, process, and organizational innovation [see e.g. Damanpour (1991)]. Most of them agree on the characteristics entered in Table 1 (Boer and During 2001).

Provided the new attributes are valued by consumers, product innovation increases their willingness to pay (WTP), creating scope for higher sales prices. This in turn permits incomes and fringe benefits for those employed in the industry to rise, causing them to welcome product innovation. In the case of process innovation, the attributes of the good do not change. However, it is produced at lower cost, which usually implies a faster work pace. Therefore, process innovation is resisted by employees but often forced upon them by international competition.

For instance, Toyota reportedly takes just 18 employee hours to manufacture a car, compared to 40 at General Motors in the 1980s. By the 2000s, General Motors was down to 20 h (Arvidson, n.d.). Finally, a typical characteristic of organizational innovation is vertical (dis)integration. A famous example is the acquisition of Fisher Body by General Motors in 1926 in order to ensure that the body shells supplied by Fisher had perfect fit (Coase 2000). Conversely, focusing on a company's core skills sometimes calls for outsourcing certain tasks to suppliers. Organizational innovation is seldom welcomed by employees, who are confronted with changes in their job content.

Turning to the healthcare industry, this categorization may explain a puzzle: Why is it that health insurers and policy makers are afraid of medical innovation whereas technological innovation is considered an important source of cost savings in the

P. Zweifel (✉)
Emeritus University of Zurich, Zurich, Switzerland
e-mail: peter.zweifel@uzh.ch

S. Walzer (ed.), *Digital Healthcare in Germany*, Contributions to Economics,
https://doi.org/10.1007/978-3-030-94025-6_3

Table 1 The three types of innovation

Type	Product innovation	Process innovation	Organizational innovation
Effect	Bestows new attributes on goods	Leaves attributes unchanged, reduces cost of production	Leaves attributes unchanged, reduces overall cost
Impact on consumers	Enhances their WTP[a]	Leaves WTP[a] unchanged	Leaves WTP[a] usually unchanged
Impact on firms	Creates scope for higher sales price	Enhances competitiveness	Enhances competitiveness
Impact on workers in the industry	Creates scope for higher wages, fringe benefits	Speeds up production process and pace of work	Frequently imposes changes in job content

[a] *WTP* Willingness to pay

remainder of the economy? It is the preponderance of costly product innovation in health care, contrary to cost-reducing process and organizational innovation. Whereas international competition forces producers to implement the latter types of innovation, this pressure is absent from healthcare providers, who are sheltered from international competition so can focus on cost-increasing product innovation. As will be shown in Sect. 2, health insurance also encourages product over process and organizational innovation.

2 Product Innovation in Health Care

According to Time Magazine (2019), there are 12 innovations that will revolutionize health care in the 2020s. Six among them (drone-delivered medical supplies, a stem-cell cure for diabetes, a wristband that can read one's mind, a pocket-size ultrasound, health care available at shopping centers,[1] and rehab in virtual reality) are product innovations directly benefiting patients sow ill enhance their willingness to pay (WTP). Deloitte (n.d.) lists ten innovations in health care, of which six again are of the product innovation type (3D-printed devices that fit patients' physiological needs, immunotherapy without negative side effects, point-of-care diagnostics, use of social media to improve patient experience, care conveniently offered at retail clinics,[2] telehealth).

Both potential and current *patients* are strongly interested in product innovation with its promise of better health outcomes (see Table 2).[3] As to *potential* patients,

[1]This could also be counted as an organizational innovation.

[2]Again, this could also be counted as an organizational innovation.

[3]The entries of Table 2 are admittedly somewhat impressionistic. In principle, they should be derived from models of behavior based on utility maximization under constraint. For instance, potential patients weigh the sacrifice of consumption possibilities against the chance of being in

Table 2 Players in the healthcare sector and their incentives to adopt the three types of innovation

Impact on ...	Product innovation	Process innovation	Organizational innovation
Patients	Strong interest, increased WTP[a]	Minimal interest, little savings	Some interest, potential savings
Physicians	Strong interest	Some interest	Resistance
Hospitals	Strong interest	Some interest	Some interest
Innovator firms[b]	Strong interest	Some interest	Little interest
Financiers (health insurers, government)	No interest	Some interest	Much interest

[a]WTP: Willingness to pay
[b]The incentives of innovator firms are evident so are not discussed any further

they need to weigh the future benefits of cost-increasing new diagnostics and therapies against the (minimal) increase in their contributions to health insurance (or in taxation in the case of a National Health Service). However, research suggests that the increase in their WTP exceeds the extra cost [see e.g. Nocera et al. (2003), Lang et al. (2011), Shaugule et al. (2015). *Current* patients benefit from the protection of health insurance, which usually burdens them with the higher cost of innovative services only through a low copayment (for an example, see Table 3).

As to *physicians*, patients' increased WTP translates into an increased demand for their services in two ways. New diagnostics and therapies hold the promise of increased success of treatment, motivating people to contact a physician to begin with and/or to continue treatment. Second, they are willing to consent to a more intensive treatment which usually goes along with increased physician earnings. This creates a strong incentive for physicians to adopt product innovation, especially in the guise of new pharmaceuticals which can be prescribed at little cost in terms of provider time.

Very much the same is true of *hospitals*, who too seek to profit from patients' increased WTP for innovative therapies. Indeed, they compete for patients importantly through the array of treatments they can offer (HealthManagement.org 2016).

This interest spills over to *innovator firms*, who find it much easier to sell product innovation (pharmaceuticals in particular) than process innovations to firms in the healthcare industry.

good health in the future, which arguably increases with product innovation in health care as soon as there may be a period of illness. The same argument olds *a fortiori* for current patients, implying that they too exhibit WTP for product innovation in health care see e.g. Zweifel et al. (2009; ch. 3.4). However, the specification of the physician utility function continues to be an open issue, as stated by Frank (2007). Similarly, Feldstein (2015, chs. 14–17) fails to find clear evidence suggesting that non-profit hospitals behave differently from for-profit ones. The objectives of (social) health insurers has been little researched; but it can be safely assumed that they want to at least break even, justifying the pertinent entries in Table 2 [see e.g. Zweifel et al. (2007)]. Finally, ever since Buchanan and Tullock (1962), political decision-makers are seen to be motivated by their chance of (re-)election, which suffers when contributions to (often compulsory) health insurance increase due to costly product innovation in health care.

Table 3 Example of a product innovation and its cost implications

Existing therapy	*Cost in $*
Time cost to patient 8 h @ $50 (assumed)	400
Maximum financial WTP of insured (assumed)	500
Maximum acceptable financial cost, rate of copayment 10%	5000
Total acceptable cost to patient	900
Total cost to financier (health insurer, government) = 0.9 × 5000	4500
Innovative therapy	
Time cost to patient 1 h @ $50 (assumed)	50
Maximum financial WTP of insured (assumed)	1000
Maximum acceptable financial cost, rate of copayment 10%	10,000
Total acceptable cost to patient (1000 + 7 × 50 time saved)	1350
Total cost to financier (health insurer, government) = 0.9 × 10,000	9000

Finally, the *financiers* (health insurers or the government, respectively in countries with a National Health Service) have no interest in product innovation; rather, they fear it. The example displayed in Table 2 shows why.

Let a patient consider a medical intervention for which he or she needs to spend a night at the hospital. Let his or her extra time input (travel, waiting, undergoing the procedure) be 8 h, valued at $50 (say). In addition to this time cost, the patient is willing to pay up $500 out of pocket for the intervention. With a copayment rat of 10%,[4] the actual financial cost of the intervention may be as high as $5000, and the patient will still opt for it (10% of 5000 equals 500). The total effective cost to the patient may thus be as high as $900 (=500 + 400) to be acceptable. The outlay for the financier (the health insurer or the government in country with a National Health Service) amounts to $4500 (=90% of 5000).

Now let there be an innovative ambulatory therapy that requires only one hour's worth of patient time while the patient is now willing to pay $1000 in view of an increased chance of successful treatment and less pain and discomfort. This means that at a copayment of 10%, the new therapy may now cost as much as $10,000, and the patient will opt for it. If in addition the patient values the avoided time input, the new therapy may even cost up to $13,500 (10% of 13,500 equals 1350).[5] Assuming that the innovative healthcare provider siphons off the entire increase in patients' WTP, the price of the treatment indeed increases to $13,500, of which the insured pays $1350 in money and $50, in time. If the provider were to charge a fee of $7000 only (say), then this cost would even fall, from $900 to $750 (=700 + 50), causing an increase in the demand for treatment—the normal demand response to a reduction in cost.

[4]Note that in many European countries, copayment is lower than 10%, especially in case of hospitalization.

[5]Even if from a purely medical viewpoint the new therapy has no value, the avoided time cost is sufficient to lead to an increase in the WTP of the patient which permits the service provider to raise its fee.

Yet for the financier, the innovative therapy is far from costless. In the extreme, its outlay increases from $4500 to $9000 (=90% of 10,000) or even $12,150 if the provider is aware of the patient's value of time. To avoid this increase, it would have to negotiate with the hospital to keep its fee constant at $5000—an unlikely outcome. On the one hand, healthcare providers want to profit from patients' increased WTP; on the other hand, the implementation of an innovation has its cost as well.

3 Process Innovation in Health Care

The list of Time Magazine (2019) cited in Sect. 2 mentions but three process innovations (Big Data covering all humanity, a comprehensive global bio bank, and a three-dimensional representation of the heart). The list put together by Deloitte (n.d.) also contains but three process innovations (Artificial intelligence, virtual reality, biosensors and trackers). This confirms the claim that health insurance coverage encourages product innovation while discouraging process innovation in healthcare. The easiest way to see this is to read Table 2 the other way round.

Let a *patient* have the choice between a conventional treatment that costs $8500 and an alternative that thanks to process innovation costs only $5000. However, with 10% copayment, 90% of the cost saving of $3500 accrues to the health insurer (the government, respectively), leaving only $350 to the patient. If the alternative is associated with seven extra hours of time input at $50 (e.g. because the healthcare provider offering it is farther away), the patient's cost saving is completely wiped out.

A *physician*'s incentive to adopt a process innovation is also limited because it does not attract additional patients or generate additional visits. What remains is the lowered variable cost of the practice, which however has to be weighed against the fixed cost of implementing the new process. In addition, workers often resent changes in process because they entail the devaluation of their specific human capital (Zwick 2002). This is especially true of employees in medical practice, who must learn in detail how the "captain of the team" wants things to be run. In addition, whereas process innovation is simply forced upon a firm by international competition (recall the auto example cited in Sect. 2), high barriers to entry shelter physician practices from competition in most industrial countries (Martins Martinho 2012).

Process innovation is of limited interest to *hospitals* as well, once again because it does not attract patients. Moreover, it may force physicians and nursing staff to perform their functions faster, opening the door to the killing argument that this results in a lower quality of treatment (Economist Intelligence Unit 2009).

This lack of interest impacts on *innovator firms*, who have difficulty selling process innovations to physician practices and hospitals (Berlin 2011).

By way of contrast, *financiers* (health insurers and governments) see the potential of purchasing health services at lower cost on behalf of consumers because process innovation permits to produce a service with unchanged characteristics at lower cost, which translates into lower prices given sufficient pressure of competition. Yet for insurers, reaping this potential would require them to be able to negotiate with select groups of physicians and hospitals, which is legally impossible in most industrial countries outside Managed Care (and the United States and the Netherlands).

4 Organizational Innovation in Health Care

Starting again with the list of Time Magazine (2019) cited in Sect. 2, one cannot find more than one item (Health care available at shopping centers) out of 12 that may count as an organizational innovation. Among the ten put together by Deloitte (n.d.), one might consider care conveniently offered at specialized clinics as an organizational innovation. This is in keeping with Richman et al. (2013), who decry the structural ossification of the healthcare industry. In stark contrast, the authors cite Apple's MP3 business model with iTunes which transformed the music business. They also note that often new entrants pose challenges that force established firms to undertake major organizational changes in order to compete in the market. However, sometimes incumbent firms do expose their divisions to internal competition, as e.g. Hewlett-Packard, who developed the ink jet printer as a competitor to its own laser jet technology.

A country's healthcare industry is sheltered from international competition through licensing requirements for almost all healthcare providers and laws regulating the staffing and location of hospitals. For instance, according to the American Hospital Association (2017) its members must abide with no fewer than 627 federal regulations.

Arguably, potential *patients* stand to benefit considerably from organizational innovation. The leading example is of course the Managed Care Organization (MCO), which combines the provision of health care with insurance. For their contribution, subscribers obtain medical services at no or only minimal copayment; in return, they are usually constrained in their choice of physician and hospital to those providers who have signed up with the MCO. Major employers in the United States are legally obliged to contract for health insurance on behalf of their workforce; they see the MCO as a way to lower their contribution to the health insurance premium.

But *current* patients have militated against the lock-in effect of MC, forcing MCOs to offer less restrictive alternatives that allow them to opt for non-contractual providers in return for an out-of-pocket payment. In Switzerland, where the choice of health insurance reflects consumer preferences without any employer involvement, health insurers offer the full range of MC alternatives, from second-opinion plans to the Health Maintenance Organization with strictly limited provider choice. Compared to conventional fee-for-service reimbursement, premiums are up to 20% lower (moneyland.ch, n.d.). The overall market share of MC currently exceeds 73% (Federal Office of Health BAG 2020).

Physicians traditionally have resisted organizational innovation in the guise of vertical integration, fearing a loss of autonomy. Indeed, Stoddard et al. (2001) found that professional autonomy is (along with relative income) one of the most important determinants of physicians' career satisfaction in the United States. An argument against MC continued to be its alleged deleterious effect on patient health (Christianson et al. 2005), although U.S. Congress had defined as early as 1986 four conditions that had to be satisfied by provisions that are likely to reduce intensity of care in Medicare-participating Health Maintenance Organizations: (1) No payments are to be made to individual physicians on the basis of their experience with individual patients; (2) The physician also is at risk for services other than his or her own; (3) The HMO provides stop-loss protection to physicians for the costs of enrollees' catastrophic illnesses; and (4) the HMO surveys enrollees periodically to ensure adequate access and satisfaction (Hillman 1991). In important cost-reducing incentive used by MCOs has been the replacement of fee-for-service payment by a fixed prospective payment per enrollee. It has been met with the criticism that such alternative forms of payment undermine medical ethics, which however does not withstand scrutiny (Zweifel and Janus 2017a, b).

Even in the case of *health insurers*, it is not always evident that they are in favor of organizational innovation in the guise of MCOs (Ehlert et al. 2017). In contradistinction to Hewlett-Packard, they may be unwilling to cannibalize their existing business model. The U.S. federal *government* showed strong interest in the cost-saving potential of organizational innovation. In 1973 already, it passed the Health Maintenance Organization Act, which requires major employers to have at least one HMO on offer. In return, qualifying HMOs must offer more comprehensive benefits than conventional plans while charging lower contributions. U.S. state governments, who are responsible for Medicaid (the scheme for the poor) have sought to relieve their budgetary burden by outsourcing to MCOs, with the result that more than two-thirds of Medicaid enrollees are covered by an MCO (Kaiser Family Foundation 2020).

5 Contribution of Information Technology (IT) to Innovation in the Healthcare Industry

According to techtarget (n.d.), IT has the benefits in health care listed in Table 4. Note that items No. 2, 4, and 6 facilitate product innovations since they are likely to enhance patients' WTP; items No. 1 and 3 facilitate process innovation and item No. 5, organizational innovation. In view of the discussion in Sects. 2–4, acceptance of IT innovations by the players in the healthcare sector is therefore predicted to be but partial.

Table 4 Benefits of IT and their relationship to types of innovation in health care

No.	Benefit of IT in health care	Type of innovation facilitated; appeal of IT to . . .
1	Ability to use data analytics and big data to effectively manage population health management programs and reduce the incidence of expensive chronic health conditions	Process; financiers
2	Use of cognitive computing and analytics to perform precision medicine tailored to individual patients	Product; patients, physicians, hospitals
3	Ability to share health data (also among academic researchers to develop new medical therapies and drugs)	Process; financiers
4	Right of patients to obtain and use their own health data and collaborate in their own care with clinicians (patient empowerment, health literacy. . .)	Product; patients, physicians, hospitals
5	Transparency and facilitated data exchange between healthcare providers	Organizational; financiers
6	Improved patient convenience (telemedicine, home delivery of pharmaceuticals, online submission of bills to health insurers, etc.)	Product; patients, physicians, hospitals

Source: techtarget (n.d.), complemented by author (see also Table 2)

5.1 IT Facilitating Product Innovation

Prediction 1 Patients' WTP is little affected by IT facilitating the product innovations listed in Table 3. This lack of interest spills over to all other players in the healthcare sector.

In Table 3, No. 2 (Use of cognitive computing and analytics to perform precision medicine tailored to individual patients) and No. 4 (Fostering the right of patients to obtain and use their own health data) do constitute product innovations that enhance *patients'* WTP. As to precision medicine in No. 2, Jain and Shah (2020) emphasize the importance of machine learning made possible only through Electronic Health Records (EHRs), which also facilitate innovation No. 4. Yet Health Inc. (2019) cites an investigation into EHRs that reports software glitches, user errors, and other system flaws that create risks to patient safety. Also, *gaps in interoperability mean that patients cannot share their* computerized medical histories throughout the healthcare sector.

In view of their limited impact on patients' WTP, *physicians* and *hospital*s also have limited incentive to adopt these types of IT innovation. In view of Table 1 above, this holds true *a priori* for *health insurers* and the *government,* who have little interest in cost-increasing product innovation. With regard to government, this prediction seems to be contradicted by the Health Information Technology for Economic and Clinical Health (HITECH) Act of 2009 as well as President Obama's Precision Medicine Initiative which again extols the benefits listed in Table 3 (White House 2015). However, Adams and Petersen (2016) have raised doubts about patients' acceptance of this innovation, citing in particular concerns about the privacy of genetic information that might be used in a discriminatory way.

5.2 IT Facilitating Process Innovation

Prediction 2 IT facilitating the process innovations listed in Table 3 are resisted by physicians and hospitals but may be welcomed by insurers and government.

As shown in Sect. 2, both potential and current *patients* have little interest in process innovation due to insurance coverage; therefore IT innovations facilitating them meet with little appeal.

Turning to *physicians*, in a study of 56 general practitioners Spil et al. (2004) found that electronic prescription systems (EPS), which correspond to innovation No. 3 in Table 3 were not used in 72% of the cases due to their resistance, which in turn was driven by a lack of relevance of the system to user needs, low degree of meeting user needs, and lack of resources to design, operate, and maintain the system. Interestingly, lack of incentives (such as saving of physician or staff time) was not cited. As a matter of fact, Cocchi (2014) emphasizes that physicians often fear a drop in their productivity, over-reliance on EHR systems, and interference with patient communication. In a multivariate statistical analysis, Barrett (2017) relates resistance against EHRs not only by physicians but also nurses and hospital employees to a number of their job characteristics. Health Inc. (2019) also reports burnouts *because physicians are* clicking pull-down menus and typing rather than interacting with patients.

Bhattacherjee and Himet (2007) point out that traditionally *hospitals* have focused on optimizing patient flow in the aim of minimizing idle time of medical and nursing staff. This reflects the view that patient time is (almost) worthless, which is increasingly being challenged because wage growth is rendering time ever more precious in the economy (Becker 1995). In response, adopting a process perspective calling for redesigning and institutionalizing a sequence of work tasks has been advocated. An important component of redesign has been Computerized Physician Order Entry (CPOE), again corresponding to item No. 3 of Table 3. However, by the mid-2000s, less than 20% of hospitals had introduced CPOE even in the United States and the Netherlands, the two most advanced countries among seven studied (Aarts and Koppel 2009). In a case study, Bygstad et al. (2017) report on the introduction of IT in a newly built Norwegian hospital. They note the continuing conflict between the process redesign and the digital infrastructure communities; the first is focused on timely launch of the innovation, while the second seeks to install a holistic IT architecture for long-term service.

Although *financiers* in principle welcome IT innovation facilitating process innovation (see entries No. 1 and 3 of Table 3), they have experienced disappointment. *Health Inc.* (2019) *reports on signs of fraud in that IT has been used by healthcare providers for* upcoding the severity of patient cases in the aim to obtain higher payment. Also, since US Medicare and Medicaid have been encouraging the use of EHR, some providers are alleged to have overstated their use of the new technology.

5.3 IT Fostering Organizational Innovation

Prediction 3 IT facilitating the organizational innovations listed in Table 3 are resisted by physicians and hospitals but welcomed by financiers.

Entry No. 5, Transparency and facilitated data exchange between healthcare providers, arguably is the one organizational innovation listed in of Table 3. It is of little relevance to *patients* (apart from possible privacy concerns). The greatest impact of IT likely is in terms of facilitating vertical integration.

Before the impact of IT innovation, a study by van Walraven et al. (2008) found that only 22% of sampled *physicians* in Canada had information about patients' previous visits at another provider. The authors conclude that the quality of care would be improved if there was more data exchange. Unfortunately, there seems to be a lack of research on physicians' attitudes toward information exchange facilitated by IT.

As to *hospitals*, a study by Wang et al. (2015) identified clear reservations among Taiwanese clinicians against facilitated data exchange between hospitals because of privacy concerns, which interestingly were of less importance to patients. Once again, there seems to be a lack of research into the acceptance of new IT designed to facilitate transparency and information exchange (item No. 5 of Table 3). One expectation is that it makes managing a hospital chain easier because headquarters obtain access to comparable operating characteristics of each unit (who however may fear a loss of autonomy). Another possibility is for *health insurers* to monitor the performance of the service providers they contract with, enabling them to act as prudent purchasers. However, this type of IT is likely to be resisted by the health professions, again for fear of losing their autonomy.

While it does not explicitly address the contribution of IT, Kaiser Permanente, a major U.S. *health insurer*, clearly fosters the exchange of data between the healthcare providers participating in its networks (Kaiser Family Foundation 2018). In the case of the United States, the federal *government* has sought to advance IT designed to enhance data exchange by creating the Office of the National Coordinator for Health Information Technology (ONC); a recent website even speaks of the "Next consumer revolution" (ONC 2017).

In all, Prediction 3 can be tested but partially at best because of a scarcity of literature addressing the role of IT in the context of organizational innovation.

6 An Additional Test: The Digital Health Care Act of Germany

On 1 January 2020, the Digital Health Care Act (DGA; Digitale-Versorgung-Gesetz, DVG in German) became law. Its objective is to provide patients with access to so-called "prescribable digital health applications" (Digitale

Gesundheitsanwendungen, DiGAs), meaning that physicians can prescribe the pertinent apps as items in the list of benefits of social health insurance. Moreover, the law makes the electronic health record (EHR, elektronische Patientenakte ePA) compulsory, also for hospitals and pharmacies. In view of the fact that the first attempt at introducing the HER occurred in 2002, it brings a protracted reform process to a head [for an historical overview, see Infografik (2021)].

This raises the question of whether this initiative will be successful in spurring the adoption of new IT by the German healthcare sector. In the case of telemedicine (No. 6 in Table 3), Brauns (2015) had complained in his 10-year anniversary presidential address to DGTelmed, the pertinent association, that the remuneration of telemonitoring in ambulatory care was still not decided and the relationship between the e-health card and telemedicine continued to be an open issue. The new law makes new IT also a *product innovation* since licensed digital health applications must be reimbursed by all social health insurers (who receive an extra compensation 300 million euros. annually of extra public funds). This may explain why the law found a majority at all in Parliament. In the past, German healthcare providers have been quick to adopt product innovations. In 2012 the country had already 17.4 Magnetic Resonance Imaging (MRI) units and 15.4 Computed Tomography (CT) scanners per million inhabitants, respectively, comparable to the United States with 18.2 and 17.0 (OECD 2020).

The fact new IT will be licensed in a fast track process by the Federal Institute for Drugs and Medical Devices (Bundesinstitut für Arzneimittel und Medizinprodukte, which roughly corresponds to the U.S. FDA) rather than the Federal association of social health insurers (GKV Bundesverband) also plays a role. The DGA of 2020 recognizes that the ability to use data analytics and big data (No. 1 in Table 3, a *process innovation)* is an important benefit that can be reaped through IT. Already before the passage of the law, no fewer than 50 IT developers of Big Data with activity in Germany were listed on the website https://www.goodfirms.co/big-data-analytics/germany. However, none of them prominently advertised a recommendation by a healthcare provider (20 of them do not have a review at all). This is going to change as more than 50 apps were already in the fast track as of 2020 (Stern et al. 2020). Resistance against facilitating the transfer of health data comes from parts of the medical profession; Enger (2020) even lodged a constitutional challenge against the Federal Ministry of Health on behalf of IG-Med, arguing that the safety and privacy of patient data are undermined by the DGA. However, according to statista (2020), no fewer than 55% of respondents expressed their confidence that regulations governing the privacy of patient data would continue to be observed.

Finally, one may ask whether the DGA might spur *organizational innovation* in German health care, the lack of which had been noted for some time (Amelung et al. 2008). A likely reason is that the German healthcare sector traditionally has been characterized by a strict separation of ambulatory and hospital care. Physicians in private practice always feared the competition by policlinics offering medical services at little or no charge. Policlinics existing in former Communist Eastern Germany quickly closed their doors after reunification in 1990 (Freudenstein and Borgwart 1992). Twenty years on, Davis et al. (2014) still ranked Germany second-lowest out of 11 OECD countries in the category 'Coordinated Care'. According to Milstein and Blankart (2016), the Health Care Strengthening Act has since advanced MC, in Germany known as 'Integrated Care'. However, an analysis of German health insurers' incentives shows that even they may hesitate to invest in MCOs and hence in IT innovation related to them (Ehlert et al. 2019). Possibly this hesitancy reflects concerns of the insured that are unlikely to be mitigated by the DGA. Indeed, the survey cited above (statista 2020) reveals that a full 52% of respondents do not envisage that new IT will improve access to medical care in rural areas. Yet centers for integrated care (which typically contract with a MCO) are concentrated in urban areas (Portal für Medizinische Versorgungszentren, n.d.). In sum, the DCA is unlikely to spur organizational innovation in German healthcare, at least in the guise of MCOs.

7 Concluding Remarks

The objective of this chapter is to identify the incentives of the major players in the healthcare sector (both potential and current patients, physicians, hospitals, health insurers, and the government as financiers) to adopt IT innovations in health care. At the outset, a distinction is made between product, process, and organizational innovation, all of which can be facilitated by IT. As to product innovation, it serves to increase both potential and current patients' willingness to pay (WTP) for treatment, which benefits physicians and hospitals by creating demand; to the extent that new IT facilitates this type of innovation, both are predicted to adopt it. By way of contrast, health insurers and governments see little advantage in IT innovation fostering costly product innovation (Prediction 1). Since cost-reducing process innovation does not affect patients' WTP, new IT enabling this type of innovation is of little interest to patients and healthcare providers. However, the financiers see the benefit of IT serving to lower the cost of health care (Prediction 2). Finally, organizational innovation, which usually goes along with vertical integration as exemplified by Managed Care, has been resisted by physicians for fear of losing their professional autonomy to health insurers. In turn, the insured as potential patients as well as health insurers and governments stand to benefit from cost reductions so have an interest in IT innovation applied to organizational restructuring (Prediction 3). The available pieces of evidence suggest that these three predictions are largely confirmed: IT innovation enabling product innovation is welcomed by healthcare providers, while IT innovation enabling process and organizational innovation is resisted by them (but welcomed by health insurers and governments). Germany's Digital Health Care Act of 2020 overcomes this resistance by making apps prescribed by healthcare providers reimbursable by social health insurers, who are compensated for their additional outlay. In fact, it treats IT innovation facilitating process and organizational innovation very much the same as a product innovation, thus paving the way for its adoption.

Acknowledgments The author would like to thank Johannes Schoder, PhD (Helsana Insurance, Switzerland) for his helpful suggestions.

References

Aarts, J., Koppel, R. (2009). Implementation of computerized physician order entry in seven countries. *Health Affairs* 28(2).

Adams, S.A., Petersen, C. (2016). Precision medicine: opportunities, possibilities, and challenges for patients and providers. *Journal of the American Medical Informatics Association* 23(4), 787-790.

Amelung, V.E., Meyer-Lutterloh, K., Schmid, E. et al. (2008). *Integrierte Versorgung und Medizinische Versorgungszentren.* (Integrated Care and Medical Service Centers), 2nd ed. Berlin: Medizinisch Wissenschaftliche Verlagsgesellschaft.

American Hospital Association (2017). *Federal Agencies with Regulatory or Oversight Authority Impacting Hospitals.* https://www.aha.org/system/files/2018-01/info-regulatory-burden-federal-agencies.pdf

Arvidson, E. (n.d.). How long does it take to build a car from start to finish? https://itstillruns.com/long-build-car-start-finish-7811332.html.

Barrett, A.K. (2017). Electronic Health Record (EHR) organizational change: Explaining resistance through profession, organizational experience, and EHR communication quality. *Health Communication* 33(4), 496-506.

Becker, G.S. (1995). A theory of the allocation of time. *Economic Journal* 75(299), 493-517.

Berlin, D.B. (2011). *Characteristics of Disruptive Innovation within the Medical Device Industry.* Cambridge: MIT MSc Thesis.

Bhattacherjee, A., Himet, N. (2007). Physicians' resistance toward healthcare information technology: A theoretical model and empirical test. *European Journal of Information Systems* 16, 725-737.

Boer, H., During, W.E. (2001). Innovation, what innovation? A comparison between product, process, and organizational innovation. *International Journal of Technology Management* 22 (1/2/3), 83-107.

Brauns, H.-J. (2015). Presidential address to DGTelmed's tenth anniversary. https://www.dgtelemed.de/downloads/10-Jahre-dgtelemed-web.pdf.

Buchanan, J.M., Tullock, G. (1962). *The Calculus of Consent: Logical Foundations of Constitutional Democracy.* Ann Arbor MI: University of Michigan Press.

Bygstad, B., Hanseth, O., Siebenherz, A., Øvrelid, E. (2017). Process innovation meets digital infrastructure in a high-tech hospital. In *Proceedings of the 25th European Conference on Information Systems (ECIS).* Guimarães, Portugal, June 5-10, 801-814.

Christianson J.B., Warrick, L.H., Wholey, D.R. (2005). Physicians' perceptions of Managed Care: A review of the literature. *Medical Care Research and Review* 62(6), 635-675.

Coase, R.H. (2000). The acquisition of Fisher Body by General Motors. *Journal of Law & Economics* 43(1), 15-32.

Cocchi, R. (2014). Physician resistance against EHR systems and how to overcome it. *Healthcare Business & Technology*, 25 March. http://www.healthcarebusinesstech.com/ehr-systems-resistance/.

Davis, K., Schoen, K.S.C., Squires, D. (2014). Mirror, mirror on the wall, 2014 update: How the U.S. health care system compares internationally. London: Commonwealth Fund.

Deloitte (n.d.). Top 10 health care innovations. https://www2.deloitte.com/global/en/pages/life-sciences-and-healthcare/articles/top-10-health-care-innovations.html

Damanpour, F. (1991). Organizational innovation: A meta-analysis of the effects and moderation. *Academy of Management Journal* 34, 555-590.

Economist Intelligence Unit (2009). *Doctor Innovation. Shaking up the Health System.* http://graphics.eiu.com/marketing/pdf/Philips_Shaking_up.pdf.
Ehlert, A., Oberschachtsiek, D., Wein, T. (2019). Factors driving German physicians' Managed Care participation. *German Economic Review* 20(2), 171-193.
Ehlert, A., Wein, T., Zweifel, P. (2017). Overcoming resistance against Managed Care – Insights from a bargaining model. *Health Economic Review* 7(1), 1-15.
Enger, I. (2020). Verfassungsklage gegen Spahns Digitale-Versorgung-Gesetz (DVG) eingereicht _ Mitdenken-761.html (Constitutional challenge lodged against (minister) Spahn's DGA), accessed 15 Aug 2021.
Federal Office of Health BAG (2020). *Statistik der Krankenversicherung* 2019, Table 7.07. https://ch.search.yahoo.com/search?fr=mcafee&type=E210CH0G0&p=statistik+der+krankenversicherung+schweiz&_guc_consent_skip=1602259467.
Feldstein, P.J. (2015). *Health Policy Issues. An Economic Perspective.* Chicago IL: Health Administration Press.
Frank, R.G. (2007). Behavioral economics and health economics. In P. Diamond and H. Vartiainen (Eds.), *Behavioral Economics and Its Applications*, Princeton NJ: Princeton University Press, ch. 6.
Freudenstein, U., Borgwart, G. (1992). Primary medical care in former East Germany: The frosty winds of change. *British Medical Journal* 304, 8279.
Health Inc. (2019). Why the promise of Electronic Health Records has gone unfulfilled. https://www.npr.org/sections/health-shots/2019/03/18/704475396/why-the-promise-of-electronic-health-records-has-gone-unfulfilled
HealthManagement.org (2016). The keys to staying competitive in today's healthcare market. https://healthmanagement.org/c/hospital/whitepaper/the-keys-to-staying-competitive-in-today-s-healthcare-market.
Hillman, A.L. (1991). Managing the physician: Rules versus incentives. *Health Affairs* 10(4).
Infografik_ Chronik der Telematik_infrastruktur – 2001 bis 2021.html, 21 July 2021, accessed on 18 Aug. 2021.
Jain, K., Shah, V. (2020). *Artificial Intelligence for Precision Medicine and Better Healthcare.* KDNuggets.com. https://www.kdnuggets.com/2020/09/artificial-intelligence-precision-medicine-better-healthcare.html.
Kaiser Family Foundation (2020). Medicaid MCO state-level enrollment data. https://www.kff.org/data-collection/medicaid-managed-care-market-tracker/.
Kaiser Family Foundation (2018). *Kaiser Permanente Health Information Exchange (HIE) Program Status.* https://www.ssa.gov/ndf/documents/Mattison%20NDF%208-22-18_Final%20Remediated_RC.pdf.
Lang, H-C., Chang, K., Ying, Y-H. (2011). Quality of life, treatments, and patients' willingness to pay for a complete remission of cervical cancer in Taiwan. *Health Economics* 21(10), 1217-1233.
Martins Martinho, A. (2012), Becoming a doctor in Europe: Objective selection systems. *AMA Journal of Ethics Virtual Mentor* 14(12), 984-988.
Milstein, R., Blankart, C.R. (2016). The Health Care Strengthening Act: The next level of Integrated Care in Germany. *Health Policy* 120(5), 445-451.
moneyland.ch (n.d.), *Swiss health insurance: Managed Care models explained.* **https://www.moneyland.ch/en/swiss-health-insurance-managed-care-models.**
Portal für medizinische Versorgungszentren (n.d.). www.mzd.de, accessed on 14 Aug. 2021.
Nocera, S., Telser, H., Bonato, D. (2003). *The Contingent-Valuation Method in Health Care: An Economic Evaluation of Alzheimer's Disease.* Dordrecht: Kluwer.
OECD Health Data (2020). https://data.oecd.org/healtheqt/.
Office of the National Coordinator for Health Information Technology (ONC) (2017). *Benefits of Health IT.* https://www.healthit.gov/topic/health-it-basics/benefits-health-it.
Richman, B. D., Mitchell, W., Schulman, K.A. (2013). Organizational innovation in health care. *Health Management, Policy and Innovation* 1(3), 36-44.

Shaugule, S.S., Hay, J., Young, G. (2015). Understanding patient preferences and willingness to pay for hemophilia therapies. *Patient Preference and Adherence* 2015(9), 1623-1630.

Spil, T.A.M., Schuring, R.W., Michel-Verkerke, M.B. (2004). Electronic prescription system: Do the professionals USE IT. *International Journal of Healthcare Technology Management* 6(1), 32–55.

statista (2020). Umfrage zur Digitalisierug im Gesundheitswesen (Survey on digitalization in the healthcare sector), Umfrage zur Digitalisierung im Gesundheitswesen _ Statista.html, accessed on 17 Aug. 2021.

Stern, A.D., Matthies, H., Hagen, J. et al. (2020). Want to see the future of digital health tools? Look to Germany. *Harvard Business Review*, 2 Dec.

Stoddard, J.J., Hargraves, J.L., Reed, M. et al. (2001). Managed care, professional autonomy, and income: Effects on physician career satisfaction. *Journal of General Internal Medicine* 16(10), 675-684.

techtarget (n.d.), *Health IT* (*health information technology*). https://searchhealthit.techtarget.com/definition/Health-IT-information-technology.

Time Magazine (2019). 12 Innovations That Will Change Health Care and Medicine in the 2020s. https://time.com/5710295/top-health-innovations/.

Van Walraven, C., Taljaard, M., Bell, C.M. et al. (2008). Information exchange among physicians caring for the same patient in the community. *Canadian Medical Association Journal* 179(10), 1013-1018.

Wang, J-Y., Hsiao, H.-Y., Chen, J-D. et al. (2015). Attitudes toward inter-hospital electronic patient record exchange: Discrepancies among physicians, medical record staff, and patients. *BMC Health Services Research* 15, No. 264.

White House (2015). *Fact Sheet: President Obama's Precision Medicine Initiative.* https://www.whitehouse.gov/the-press-office/2015/01/30/fact-sheet-president-obama-s-precision-medicine-initiative.

Zweifel, P., Breyer, F., Kifmann, M. (2009). *Health Economics*, 2nd.ed. New York: Springer.

Zweifel, P., Janus (2017a). Medical ethics: Enhanced or undermined by modes of payment? *European Journal of Health Economics* 18(1), 119-129.

Zweifel, P., Janus, K. (2017b). Reply to commentary on: Medical ethics: Enhanced or undermined by modes of payment? *European Journal of Health Economics* 18(1), 133-134.

Zweifel, P. Krey, B.B. Tagli, M. (2007). Supply of private voluntary health insurance in low-income countries. In A. S. Preker et al. (Eds.), *Private Voluntary Health Insurance in Development – Friend or Foe?* Washington: The World Bank, 55-113.

Zwick, T. (2002). Employee resistance against innovations. *International Journal of Manpower* 23(6), 542-552.

Digital Health Applications: DiGAs—Pathway to Reimbursement

Stefan Walzer and Jan-Marc Hodek

Looking at the concept of digitalisation in healthcare, it can be said that digital healthcare encompasses various areas. On the one hand, it creates new diagnostic and treatment options, such as personalised medicine, and on the other hand, it enables easier communication between the individual actors in the healthcare system. In addition, the individual patient can control his or her health better, for example through apps. Digitisation in the healthcare sector creates the opportunity to counteract the shortage of skilled workers and to relieve doctors and nurses, for example in administrative activities and documentation, diagnostics and everyday practical activities (Cf. PricewaterhouseCoopers GmbH n.d.).

When it comes to digitalisation in the health sector, Germany lags far behind. In the Bertelsmann Foundation's international comparative study, Germany ranked 16th out of 17 countries (Cf. Bertelsmann Stiftung 2018, p. 1). While video consultations and electronic patient records are standard in other European countries, many possibilities and the associated opportunities of digital innovations in the healthcare system are hardly used in Germany. Although there are some innovative ideas and approaches, these have often not been part of the standard service of statutory health insurance before the introduction of the DiGA pathway. This is also shown by the DIGITAL economic index of the Federal Ministry for Economic Affairs and Energy (BMWi), which measures sector-specific progress in digital

S. Walzer (✉)
MArS Market Access & Pricing Strategy GmbH, Weil am Rhein, Germany

State University Baden-Wuerttemberg, Lörrach, Germany

RWU – Ravensburg-Weingarten University of Applied Sciences, Weingarten, Germany
e-mail: Stefan.walzer@marketaccess-pricingstrategy.de

J.-M. Hodek
RWU – Ravensburg-Weingarten University of Applied Sciences, Weingarten, Germany
e-mail: hodek@rwu.de

S. Walzer (ed.), *Digital Healthcare in Germany*, Contributions to Economics,
https://doi.org/10.1007/978-3-030-94025-6_4

transformation. Here, the healthcare sector scored comparatively poorly in 2018 with 37 out of 100 points (Cf. Pfannstiel et al. 2020, p. 254).

To ensure that the development of digitalisation in the health sector in Germany progresses more quickly, the Federal Ministry has adopted some legal measures. These include, for example, the Digital Health Care Act (DVG) which includes reimbursement of costs for health apps, promotion of telemedical services and expansion of the telematics infrastructure.

1 What Is the DiGA System and How Does It Work?

With the entry into force of the Digital Healthcare Act on 19 December 2019, the "app on prescription" for patients was introduced into healthcare, thus laying an important foundation for advancing digital health care in Germany. According to § 33a SGB V, a DiGA is a class I or IIa medical device according to MDR or MDD. These are products with CE-marking and with a low risk of potential harm caused by a defect or functional failure of the medical device; for example as a web-application for the treatment of phobias (Velibra) or an app for the treatment of sleep disorders (Somnio). A DiGA must have the following characteristics:

- The main function relies mainly on digital technologies;
- The medical purpose is essentially achieved through the main digital function;
- The DiGA supports the detection, monitoring, treatment or mitigation of disease or disability;
- The DiGA is used by the patient or by the healthcare provider and the patient together (Cf. BfArM 2021).

A patient-relevant procedural and structural improvement is said to exist if the patient is able to cope better in everyday life with the help of the digital health application, for example. This is because it reminds him or her to take medication, supports family caregivers in providing care, or improves the exchange between doctors, caregiver and patients (Bundesinstitut für Arzneimittel und Medizinprodukte 2021).

For this purpose, the German Federal Institute for Drugs and Medical Devices (BfArM) provides a register that lists those digital applications that have successfully passed the assessment for reimbursable DiGA (Bundesinstitut für Arzneimittel und Medizinprodukte 2021). Only those DiGA that have been classified for the official list by the BfArM are then included in the reimbursement system of statutory health insurance. The digital health applications must have successfully passed a procedure at the BfArM and be listed in a newly created directory of reimbursable digital health applications, named "DiGA-Verzeichnis".[1] The application procedure is designed as a fast-track and takes a maximum of 3 months after receipt of the complete application. After that, the manufacturer can enter price negotiations with the Head Association of Health Insurance Funds (GKV-SV). Important for a successful

[1] The current list is available at: https://diga.bfarm.de/de

assessment by the BfArM is proof of a positive healthcare effect, but also product characteristics such as data protection and user-friendliness (Cf. BMG 2020).

According to the definition in the Digital Healthcare Act, positive health care effects (benefits) are either a medical benefit or patient-relevant structural and procedural process improvements in healthcare. To prove the benefit, a manufacturer must submit the results of clinical studies in the form of the final clinical study report, which must be drawn up according to recognised scientific standards. In the comparative study it must be shown that using the DiGA is better than not using it (Cf. BfArM 2021, S. 82 ff). Medical benefit means that the digital healthcare application has a positive influence on patient-relevant outcomes such as morbidity, mortality or health-related quality of life. For example, the use of a DiGA can extend a patient's life or shorten the course of the disease. Health applications with positive outcomes in the area of patient-relevant structural and procedural improvements strengthen the role of patients in their own course of therapy by improving the coordination of treatment between care providers and patients, which makes the patient's own situation more understandable, and increases the patient's participation. Health-related outcomes must be provided by means of a study conducted in Germany, which demonstrates that application has more advantages than non-application would have (Bundesinstitut für Arzneimittel und Medizinprodukte 2021).

In order to be included in the DiGA register of the BfArM, the digital health application must meet the aforementioned requirements. For this purpose, the manufacturer submits proof to the BfArM that the DiGA fulfils all requirements under medical device law. To guarantee the manufacturer's commitment to data protection laws and handling of patient information, evidence and declarations must be submitted (Bundesinstitut für Arzneimittel und Medizinprodukte 2021). General requirements also include interoperability of the technical requirements, robustness against disruptions, user-friendliness for people of all ages, quality of the medical content while maintaining the professional standards from medical guidelines, and patient safety (Bundesinstitut für Arzneimittel und Medizinprodukte 2021).

Depending on whether or not a comparative study and corresponding evidence of a positive outcome is already available for the DiGA, the manufacturer decides whether to apply for provisional or final inclusion in the BfArM listing. Without a suitable study, there can only be an application for provisional inclusion. In this case, proof of positive outcomes must be submitted subsequently at the end of the trial period. Only then does the final assessment by the BfArM begin. However, if the manufacturer immediately submits an application for final inclusion, there is no trial period and review of the submitted documents begins (Bundesinstitut für Arzneimittel und Medizinprodukte 2021).

The entire process from application to inclusion in the DiGA register and thus reimbursement by the statutory health insurance is called 'fast-track procedure'. The evaluation time by the BfArM is only 3 months. Once the application documents are fully submitted, a 3-month processing period begins. The BfArM's task is to review the manufacturer's information regarding the requirements for the DiGA and to assess the submitted proof of positive health outcomes (Bundesinstitut für Arzneimittel und Medizinprodukte 2021). The following figures illustrates the fast-track process (Figs. 1 and 2).

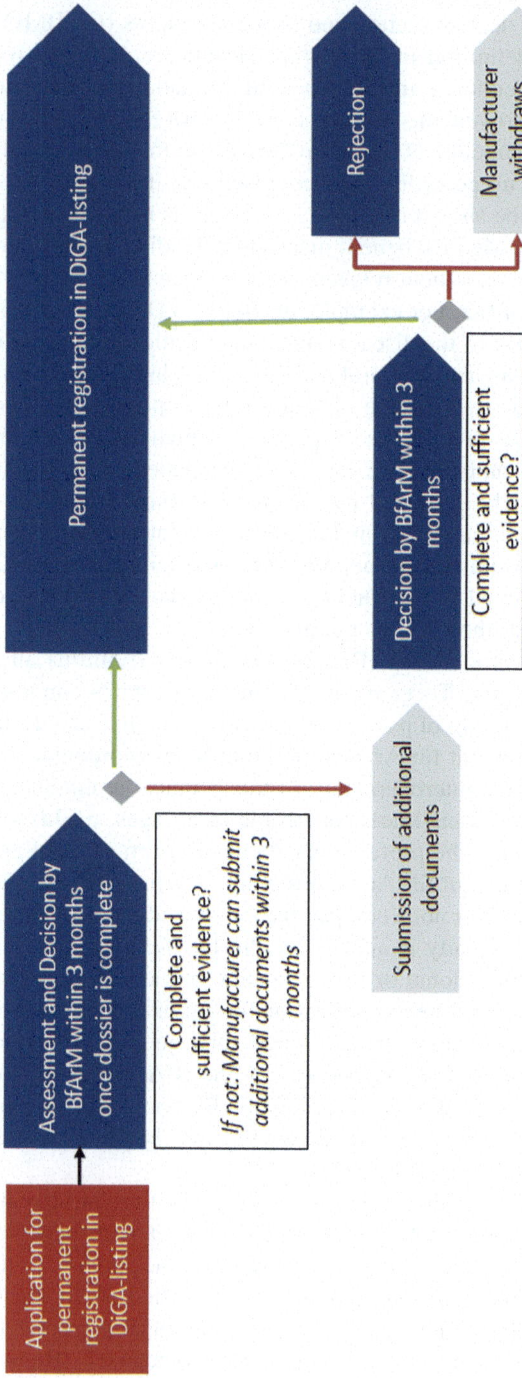

Fig. 1 Process of permanent registration in DiGA-listing

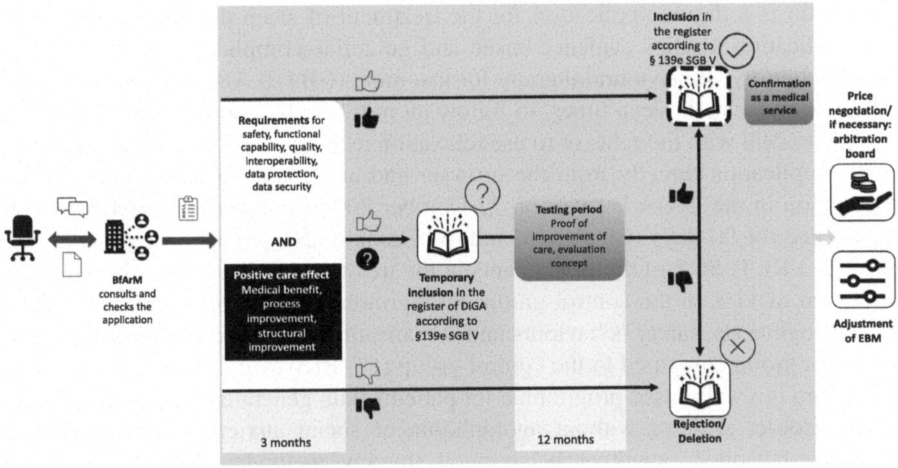

Fig. 2 Process of preliminary registration in DiGA-listing

The number of digital health applications that can be prescribed is growing rapidly. The applications officially listed by the BfArM and, therefore, eligible for prescription currently focus primarily on the indications migraine, multiple sclerosis, panic and anxiety disorders/phobias, tinnitus, depression, insomnia, obesity and coxarthrosis.

Three DiGAs have already proven the benefit by means of studies and are permanently registered in the DiGA registry:

- Elevida (multiple sclerosis)
- Somnio (non-organic insomnia)
- Velibra (phobias).

Elevida is a digital health app for people with multiple sclerosis who also have fatigue and are at least 18 years old. Elevida aims to reduce fatigue. The programme is to be used in addition to an otherwise usual treatment (for example by a GP or specialist). Elevida is based on established psychotherapeutic approaches and procedures, especially cognitive behavioural therapy (CBT). Elevida is intended for self-administration by the patient for 180 days. First registration in the DiGA list was on 15 December 2020. Elevida costs 743.75 Euros per licence for 90 days (Cf. BfArM n.d.-a). The main outcome of the elevida RCT revealed that the combination of elevida and usual medical treatment led to a significantly greater reduction in fatigue than the usual medical treatment alone by patients with multiple sclerosis who also suffered from fatigue. Furthermore, the combination led to a significant reduction in anxiety symptoms and a significant improvement in certain aspects of disease-related quality of life: fatigue, thinking ability, and leg mobility. Furthermore, the combination treatment led to significantly improved management of activities of daily living (Cf. BfArM n.d.-a).

Somnio is a digital application for the treatment of sleep disorders (insomnia). The application teaches evidence-based and guideline-compliant content from the field of cognitive behavioural therapy for insomnia (CBT-I). Users learn, for example, to optimise their sleep times, to follow an individually coordinated sleep-wake rhythm, to deal with thoughts or to use relaxation techniques. Somnio is available as a web application directly from the browser and as an app for smartphones. First registration in the DiGA list was on 22 October 2020. Somnio costs 464.00 Euros per licence for 90 days (Cf. BfArM n.d.-b). Somnio also proved a large treatment effect in a RCT: 56% of the participants in the treatment group achieved remission, compared to 11% in the control group. Furthermore, depression symptoms, sleep-related cognitions, safety behaviours and somatisation decreased significantly in the treatment group compared to the control group (Cf. BfArM n.d.-b).

Velibra is a web-based programme for patients with generalised anxiety disorder, panic disorder with or without agoraphobia or social anxiety disorder. Velibra teaches established cognitive behavioural therapy methods and exercises. The programme is intended as a supplement to a usual treatment for patients aged at least 18 years old. The prescription period for velibra is 90 days. To stabilise the effects, use for 180 days is recommended. First registration in the DiGA list was on 01.10.2020. Velibra costs 476.00 Euros per licence for 90 days (Cf. BfArM n.d.-c). The RCT of Velibra showed that the combination of Velibra and standard GP care led to significantly lower anxiety and depressive symptoms in patients with generalised anxiety disorder, panic disorder with or without agoraphobia or social anxiety disorder than usual GP care alone. The effects were detectable for up to 6 months (Cf. BfArM n.d.-c).

If the manufacturer cannot provide sufficient evidence of the positive supply effects of the DiGA, but still fulfils all other requirements, the manufacturer is allowed to submit an application for preliminary inclusion in the registry. The necessary comparative study, that demonstrates the positive effect can then be conducted within a period of up to 1 year. Exceptions allow a 2-year period. Furthermore, the manufacturer must set the price for the DiGA during the trial period. There are seven applications in the preliminary DiGA list at the beginning of 2021: Invirto, Kalmeda, M-sense, Rehappy, Selfapy, Vivira and Zanadio.

Invirto enables people with agoraphobia, panic disorder or social phobia to treat their anxiety disorder from home. Patients learn from therapists or doctors accompanied by an app and virtual reality glasses to understand their anxiety better, to cope with high levels of tension, to manage anxious thoughts and to revisit anxious situations. The accompaniment of psychotherapists or doctors ensures high-quality care and supports the users. Invirto makes it possible to reduce the symptoms of the anxiety disorder, to reduce avoidance behaviour and to regain more freedom of movement in everyday life. Invirto is based on cognitive behavioural therapy. First registration in the DiGA list was on 3 December 2020. Invirto costs 428.40 Euros (with hardware) (Cf. BfArM n.d.-d).

Kalmeda offers patients (over the age of 18) with chronic tinnitus a guideline-based, behavioural therapy. The structured programme is supplemented by relaxation instructions, soothing nature and background sounds as well as a knowledge section. The behavioural therapy programme, which lasts several months, consists of five levels with nine stages each and shows patients step by step the way to a self-determined handling of the tinnitus and to a reduction of the tinnitus burden. First registration in the DiGA list was on 25 September 2020. Kalmeda costs 116.97 Euros per licence for 90 days (Cf. BfArM n.d.-e).

M-sense offers a comprehensive digital treatment programme for migraine patients. The application includes a digital headache diary and guideline-compliant procedures for migraine prophylaxis and acute treatment of attacks. Migraine patients can access customised knowledge transfer, animated physiotherapeutic exercises, instructions for endurance sports as well as audio files for relaxation and imagination exercises. The documentation of lifestyle factors in the diary enables individual trigger management. First registration in the DiGA list was on 16 December 2020. M-sense costs 219.99 Euros per licence for 90 days (Cf. BfArM n.d.-f).

The digital health application **Rehappy** supports the follow-up care of stroke patients. Support takes the form of an individually compiled supply of motivation and knowledge with a mobile app, an activity tracker and a web portal. Patients are activated, informed and accompanied to be able to tackle their path to recovery in a sustained, self-determined, competent and confident manner. Support is based on educational information and positive reinforcement for the perception of personal responsibility and an increase in therapy adherence as well as intrinsic motivation. The prescription period for Rehappy is 90 days. With the first prescription, the activity tracker belonging to the digital health application is sent to the patient. No co-payment is required. In order to sustain the effects, it is recommended to use Rehappy for longer than the minimum prescription period. First registration in the DiGA list was on 29 December 2020. Rehappy costs 449.00 Euros per licence for the first 90 days (with hardware) and 299.00 Euros for the next 90 days (Cf. BfArM n.d.-g).

Selfapy offers depression sufferers an individual online course based on evidence-based theories and cognitive behavioural therapy techniques. Patients can follow the therapeutic content on the internet-based course on their own. The course is divided into individual lessons. Each lesson deals with one topic, such as dealing with negative thoughts, sleep problems, which creates a positive daily structure, relaxation techniques and prevention strategies. Content is taught with the help of audio and video clips, texts and exercises. Contents are individually adapted to the person's personal situation. To ensure patient safety, the patient is monitored by a personal psychologist. In case of acute need, the psychologist is available via a message function to answer questions about the application. Preliminary results from 401 participants in a study with the Charité Berlin show a significant reduction in depressive symptoms after completion of the 12-week course. First registration in the DiGA list was on 16 December 2020. Selfapy costs 540.00 Euros per licence for 90 days and access to the content for a total of 12 months (Cf. BfArM n.d.-h).

Vivira is a digital health app for the treatment of back, knee and hip pain, non-specific low back pain, osteochondrosis, osteoarthritis of the knee and hip. The Vivira movement therapy app offers four daily exercises that continuously adjust their intensity and complexity based on feedback from the patient. Daily exercises are supported by weekly health questionnaires, progress monitoring, monthly exercise tests and educational content. The effectiveness of Vivira has already been investigated in a retrospective controlled study. Patients who used Vivira showed a significant intra-individual reduction in pain. The study will be completed with a prospective randomised controlled trial and another retrospective study in 2021. First registration in the DiGA list was on 22 October 2020. Vivira costs 239.97 Euros per licence for 90 days (Cf. BfArM n.d.-i).

Zanadio is an application that helps users to reduce their weight in the long term by changing their habits in terms of exercise, nutrition and other behaviours. The DiGA is based on the scientific concept of multimodal, conservative obesity therapy, which focuses on the various relevant areas and thereby brings permanent weight reduction in the long-term. First registration in the DiGA list was on 22 October 2020. Zanadio costs 499.80 Euros per licence for 90 days (Cf. BfArM n.d.-j).

The costs of an approved digital health application will be reimbursed by the statutory health insurance if a doctor's prescription is available (or if there is a direct application to the health insurer and this insurer agrees). If the application is approved, the health insurer sends an activation code and further instructions on how to obtain the DiGA directly to the insured person. The activation marks the start of the usage period and the manufacturer settles the costs directly with the health insurance (Fig. 3).

According to current status, health insurers must reimburse the price set by the manufacturer for all approved DiGA for the first year. During this first year (after inclusion of the DiGA in the register), the price set by the manufacturer is not questioned. From the 13th month onwards, the reimbursement amount negotiated between health insurers and the manufacturer then applies. If no agreement can be reached, an arbitration board must determine the reimbursement payment. It is

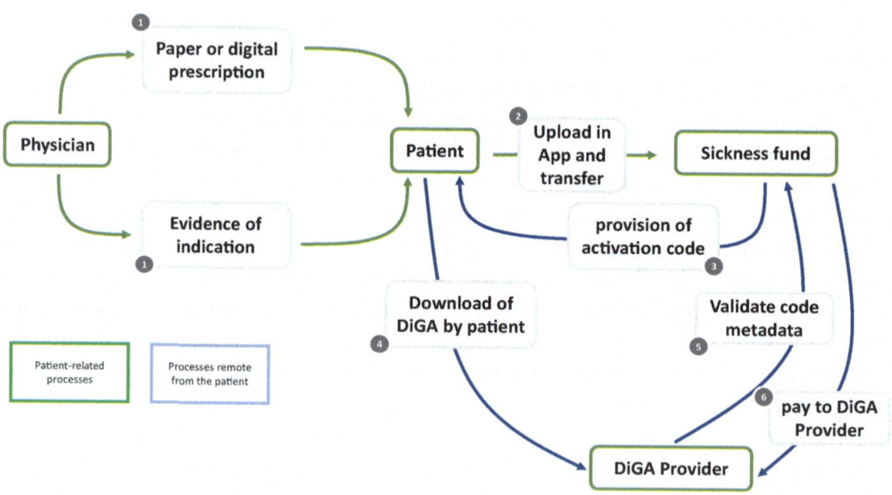

Fig. 3 Prescription process

stipulated by law that medical services associated with use of the DiGA are also reimbursed by health insurers.

What is the appropriate price? The same evidence requirements must also apply to DiGA as to other services paid by the health insurance. Currently, the requirements for proof of benefits of a DiGA are comparatively low. In future, it would be conceivable that—similar to the German reference price system for pharmaceuticals—maximum amounts for groups of comparable applications could also be set for DiGAs.

2 How Do Private Health Insurances (PKV) Manage DiGAs?

First of all a DiGA must be prescribed also for a privately insured patient. The privately insured person is well advised to ask their private health insurance (PKV) whether the costs of the DiGA will be reimbursed before making any advance payments. Obviously, DiGAs cannot be explicitly covered by the insurance contracts of the existing insured, simply because DiGAs have only been around for a short time. In principle, a private health insurance company cannot intervene in the contracts of the existing insured. So "pacta sunt servanda" applies. For reasons of antitrust law, the PKV association cannot bring about a generally applicable regulation. The same applies to the so-called "Beihilfe". The "Beihilfe" subsumes DiGAs to the aids § 25 Bundesbeihilfeverordnung (BBhV). The respective relevant annex is Annex 11 which however does not yet include any DiGAs. However, in the context of the "Beihilfe" it has been decided that digital health applications may be reimbursed in individual cases for up to 12 months. The prerequisites for recognition are the prescription of a doctor or psychotherapist and the approval of the digital health application by the BfArM in the DiGA registry. Once the insured's PKV has agreed to reimburse the costs, the insured person pays themselves and submits the bill for reimbursement to their PKV.

References

Bertelsmann Stiftung (Hrsg.). Thiel R, Deimel L, Schmidtmann D, Piesche K, Hüsing T, Rennoch J, Stroetmann V, Stroetmann K, Kostera T. (2018): #SmartHealthSystems - Digitalisierungsstrategien im internationalen Vergleich. https://www.bertelsmann-stiftung.de/de/publikationen/publikation/did/smarthealthsystems (last accessed February 23 2022)

BfArM. (n.d.-a): https://diga.bfarm.de/de/verzeichnis/419 (last accessed February 23 2022)

BfArM. (n.d.-b): https://diga.bfarm.de/de/verzeichnis/508 (last accessed February 23 2022)

BfArM. (n.d.-c): https://diga.bfarm.de/de/verzeichnis/316 (last accessed February 23 2022)

BfArM. (n.d.-d): https://diga.bfarm.de/de/verzeichnis/300 (last accessed February 23 2022)

BfArM. (n.d.-e): https://diga.bfarm.de/de/verzeichnis/350 (last accessed February 23 2022)

BfArM. (n.d.-f): https://diga.bfarm.de/de/verzeichnis/315 (last accessed February 23 2022)

BfArM. (n.d.-g): https://diga.bfarm.de/de/verzeichnis/691 (last accessed February 23 2022)
BfArM. (n.d.-h): https://diga.bfarm.de/de/verzeichnis/876 (last accessed February 23 2022)
BfArM. (n.d.-i): https://diga.bfarm.de/de/verzeichnis/387 (last accessed February 23 2022)
BfArM. (n.d.-j): https://diga.bfarm.de/de/verzeichnis/294 (last accessed February 23 2022)
Bundesministerium für Gesundheit. (2020): Verordnung über das Verfahren und die Anforderungen zur Prüfung der Erstattungsfähigkeit digitaler Gesundheitsanwendungen in der gesetzlichen Krankenversicherung (Digitale Gesundheitsanwendungen- Verordnung – DiGAV. https://www.gesetze-im-internet.de/digav/DiGAV.pdf (last accesses February 23 2022)
Bundesinstitut für Arzneimittel und Medizinprodukte. (2021): Das Fast-Track-Verfahren für digitale Gesundheitsanwendungen (DiGA) nach § 139e SGB V Ein Leitfaden für Hersteller, Leistungserbringer und Anwender. https://www.bfarm.de/SharedDocs/Downloads/DE/Medizinprodukte/diga_leitfaden.html;jsessionid=6E16D8393937F616233F46B27FCAD657.internet561?nn=597198 (last accessed February 23 2022)
PricewaterhouseCoopers GmbH. (n.d.): Digitalisierung im Gesundheitswesen, URL: https://www.pwc.de/de/gesundheitswesen-undpharma/digitalisierung-im-gesundheitswesen.html, 30.08.2020.
Pfannstiel, M., Kassel, K., Rasche, C. (2020): Innovationen und Innovationsmanagement im Gesundheitswesen, Technologien, Produkte und Dienstleistungen voranbringen, Wiesbaden: Springer

Inpatient Market Access for Digital Health Care

Stefan Walzer and Roman Spelsberg

1 Digital Transformation in German Hospitals

In contrast to other countries, like the Netherlands, Denmark or Sweden, German hospitals are not solely designed as a maximum care provider with several specialized facilities. The landscape of German hospitals is rather diverse. Hospital structures range from private hospital chains such as Helios, Asklepios or Sana, over large university hospitals to smaller hospitals (Klauber et al. 2019). Several studies claim that the number of hospitals in relation to the amount of inhabitants is too high to be able to guarantee sustainable funding and a high quality of care in all facilities (Loos et al. 2019). Strict separation of the in- and outpatient sector in Germany is also unique. Both sectors are steered with individual regulatory frameworks for the organization, funding and delivery of care. Thus, connection of the in- and outpatient sector e.g. in the form of integrated care models is particularly challenging (Pfannstiel/Jaeckel/da Cruz 2020).

At the moment an increasing number of German hospitals are going out of kilter for several reasons. For years the investment deficit has increased, which results in a crumbling infrastructure. Last year the German healthcare system experienced a switch from the inpatient sector to the outpatient sector. This trend was accelerated by the COVID-19 pandemic and resulted in lower patient numbers for hospitals. On top of these difficult circumstances, there is an urgent need for hospitals to break out

S. Walzer (✉)
MArS Market Access & Pricing Strategy GmbH, Weil am Rhein, Germany

State University Baden-Wuerttemberg, Lörrach, Germany

RWU – Ravensburg-Weingarten University of Applied Sciences, Weingarten, Germany
e-mail: Stefan.walzer@marketaccess-pricingstrategy.de

R. Spelsberg
MArS Market Access & Pricing Strategy GmbH, Weil am Rhein, Germany
e-mail: roman.spelsberg@marketaccess-pricingstrategy.de

S. Walzer (ed.), *Digital Healthcare in Germany*, Contributions to Economics,
https://doi.org/10.1007/978-3-030-94025-6_5

of traditional thought patterns and facilitate the paradigm shift in care delivery by means of innovative services such as co-creation of human and digital infrastructure. Especially in the inpatient sector digital transformation holds great promise to increase the quality of care. Opportunities arise here for patient safety, if medication errors can be prevented through automated and organized medication management systems. Furthermore, the real time collection, processing and central storage of patient data can enhance treatment decisions and support the patient through their entire journey in the hospital. Another promise digital transformation holds is the chance to finally connect the in- and outpatient sector, enable data transfer across these sectoral borders and, therefore, implement truly patient centred care. The sought after mindset for care delivery in Germany within the next 10 years will be digital care before outpatient care before inpatient care. Digital solutions will serve as support instruments for physicians and do not replace them. Moreover, this does not mean that hospitals will become redundant, but reinforces the perception that hospitals need to digitize to remain competitive.

2 Current Digitalization Level

Out of the variety of measurement instruments for the digital status of hospitals, the Electronic Medical Records Adoption Model (EMRAM) is probably the most recognized in Germany. This model was created in 2005 and stages hospitals on a scale from 0 to 7. In 2017 German hospitals had an average EMRAM-Score of 2.3. This value was calculated based on a total of 167 hospitals that have been certified since 2014. Prerequisites for stage 2 are that hospitals have a single clinical data repository (CDR), into which all orders and results are drawn up so staff do not have to sign into other systems to see results. Thus, the CDR can be regarded as a precursor to the electronic health record (EHR). Based on this data collection German hospitals can be classified as underdeveloped, compared to other countries. The fact that approximately 40% of hospitals taking part in Germany were not yet working digitally at the time of data collection in 2017, and thus landed on level 0 of the scale, is dramatic. Table 1 provides a definition for each individual level and shows the shares of hospitals in the respective levels across Germany, Europe and the USA. Figure 1 shows how the average EMRAM score evolved in Germany compared to other selected countries. From 2012 to 2017 the digital transformation of German hospitals was stagnating, while other countries like the USA recorded significant increases in average EMRAM scores. A detailed look at the shares of hospitals in each individual level in 2012 compared to 2017 underlines the fact that German hospitals are still struggling with implementation of basic digital infrastructure, while hospitals in the USA work on the connectivity of all implemented solutions and, therefore, attain higher levels (see Fig. 2).

In addition to the external, international view on the current level of digitalization in German hospitals, initiatives try to analyse the underlying reasons for the gradual process from an internal perspective. The German Physicians Union (Marburger

Table 1 EMRAM model with individual criteria and share of German, European and USA hospitals (2017), based on Klauber et al. (2019)

	Explanation	Germany	Europe	USA
N	Number of hospitals included in the evaluation	167	1455	5487
Level 7	Seamless electronic patient records integrated in all clinical areas (e.g. outpatient department, intensive care unit, emergency room) replacing all (medical) paper records; use of standards for data exchange for integrated care; data warehouse as basis for clinical and operational analyses.	–	0.3	6.4
Level 6	Clinical documentation interacts with intelligent clinical decision support (based on discrete data elements) AND the presence of an IT-supported closed loop medication process.	1.2	13.4	33.8
Level 5	Integrated image management solution (e.g. PACS) replaces all film-based images.	18.0	30.0	32.9
Level 4	Electronic prescribing with clinical decision support in at least one clinical area and for medication.	5.4	4.9	10.2
Level 3	IT-supported clinical documentation and the use of electronic prescriptions by doctors and nursing staff. This also includes the documentation of medication administration (eMAR).	9.0	5.2	12.0
Level 2	An electronic patient record (or clinical data repository) enables the aggregation and normalization of data from different clinical sources across the hospital.	26.9	28.8	1.8
Level 1	Information systems for the large diagnostic and supply departments (laboratory, radiology, pharmacy) are installed.	1.2	6.0	1.5
Level 0	Information systems for the large diagnostic and supply departments (laboratory, radiology, pharmacy) are not installed.	38.3	11.4	1.4
EMRAM average		2.3	3.6	5.3

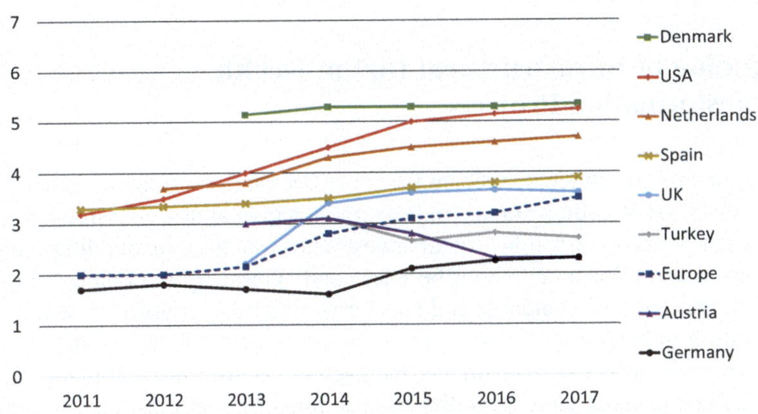

Fig. 1 Average EMRAM values in selected regions since 2011, based on Klauber et al. (2019)

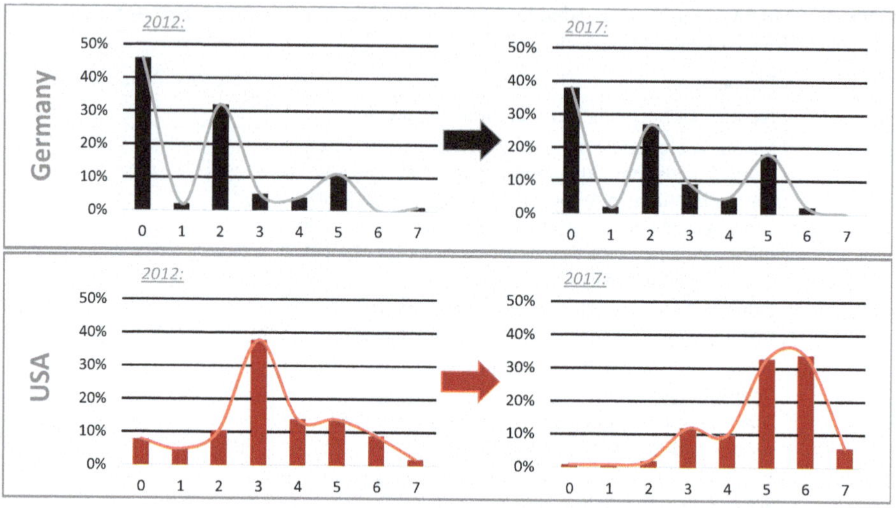

Fig. 2 EMRAM profile Germany 2012 (n = 340) vs. 2017 (n = 167) and USA 2012 (n = 5458) vs. 2017 (n = 5487), based on Klauber et al. (2019)

Bund) and the Federal Association Health IT (bvitg) initiated in 2019 a joint analyses tool named Check It to systematically collect hospital physicians' point of view on the digital transformation process in German hospitals and identify the major hurdles for adoption of digitalization projects. The physicians point out that hospitals lack fundamental digital infrastructure. One of the main weak points is communication and data transfer between departments even within one inter-physician department, which could be improved by mobile devices for physicians and the necessary applications. Furthermore, the hospitals lack qualified IT-personnel to develop and execute a digital strategy. Thus, it is not rare that medically educated personnel need to step into digital roles.

3 Funding of Infrastructural Digital Health Transformation Projects

The financing of investments in recent years has declined, resulting in an investment backlog of at least 30 billion euros. An investment gap of almost four million euros is created each year. As a result, urgent investments, such as in buildings, medical technology and digitization, cannot be made and "Germany is in danger of losing touch with international standards and lags far behind other countries when it comes to digitization in healthcare." Due to the withdrawal of the federal states, hospitals often have to finance the investments themselves. Before the following chapters provide a more detailed view on individual funding opportunities, Fig. 3 introduces the major funding mechanism for digital infrastructure projects on a macro-, meso-, and micro-level.

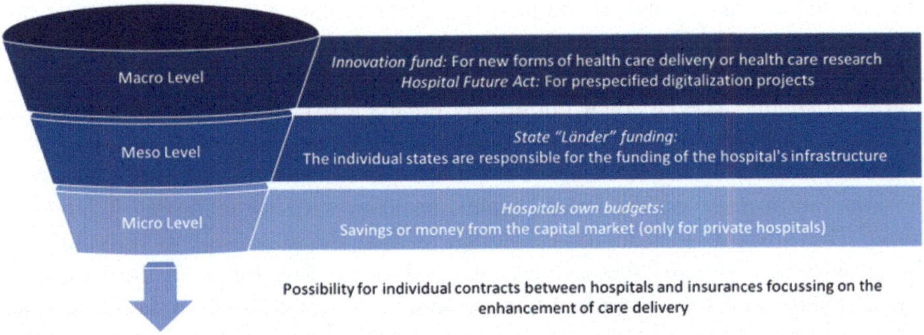

Fig. 3 Major funding options for infrastructural digital health transformation projects in Germany

3.1 Funding on a Macrolevel: Innovation fund and Hospital Future Act

The Federal Joint Committee (G-BA) has the mandate to promote new forms of healthcare delivery that go beyond the current standard provision of statutory health insurance, and healthcare research projects aimed at gaining knowledge to improve existing healthcare. For this purpose, the German federal government has set up an innovation fund. The aim of the innovation fund is to further develop the quality of care in the statutory health insurance system in Germany. In principle it is possible to apply for financing of digital transformation projects through this fund. In order to be eligible for funding the digitalization projects need to improve service delivery e.g. as a cross-sectoral care pathway. Since it is difficult to outline how digitalization projects will enhance service delivery outside the hospital setting, this fund is rarely used in this context.

Since funding opportunities on a macro level have a very bureaucratic nature, it is questionable whether these are suitable for digitalization projects. In order to be able to receive funds on a national level, the hospitals have to present a detailed plan how they are going to implement the project in their application. Thus, these funds do not allow for adjustments on the means of implementation and are not suitable for digital transformation sprints.

3.2 Hospital Future Act for the Digitalization of Hospitals

The Hospital Future Act is a law, which entails a funding programme designed to counteract the investment backlog of German hospitals. The federal government is making financial resources of three billion euros available to hospitals, which will be financed via the liquidation reserve of the healthcare fund. Although the law only came into force in 2020, its origins date back to well before the COVID-19 pandemic. It is, therefore, not a targeted distribution of economic stimulus money, but a deliberate and planned initiative by the German government to close the digitalization gap as quickly and sustainably as possible. These funds are to be used primarily for the integration of modern emergency capacities and the digitization of hospitals. The Hospital Future Act entails a list with all possible areas for funding. Hospitals seeking funding through this law need to outline how they will improve the areas specified in Table 2. In addition to the financial resources out of the liquidation reserves, the federal states are to provide up to further 1.3 billion euros. The law provides for co-financing, so that the states are to bear 30% of the planned investments themselves, either alone or together with the hospitals. The hospitals report their funding requirements to the states, which then select the projects to be funded. There is no entitlement to the funding.

Although this fund primarily focuses on the hospital infrastructure, a central point is the improved interoperability across sectors and the processes within the hospital. The law outlines the necessary interfaces (e.g. HL7), which need to be used for all digitalization projects that seek funding through this fund. The goal is to be able to connect all entities to the hospital information system and electronic patient file. In addition to the financial incentives provided through the hospital future act, the government also introduced penalties, if hospitals do not achieve a required minimum stage of digitalization. Ultimately this means that hospitals not able to achieve the minimum standard of digitalization will not be competitive any longer. The minimum standard of digital infrastructure for hospitals entails the areas outlined in Table 2. The Hospital Future Act also outlines an evaluation concept to analyse the current digitalization status of hospitals and their development over time. It is not specified yet, which scale will be used for this evaluation. The responsible government bodies classify the EMRAM-scale, which was introduced earlier in this chapter. The evaluation process will also analyse the adoption of individual projects. It is very likely, that the evaluation concept will be based on the funding areas specified in Table 2. One major hurdle for the digitalization in German hospitals will not be solved through this new law: lack of qualified IT-personnel. The funds cannot be used to finance IT-personnel, but they can be used to promote education as part of a broader digitalization project. Thus, hospitals need to cope with this hurdle by themselves.

3.3 Funding on a Meso-Level Through State Funds

Another opportunity to fund infrastructural digital health transformation projects is the application for state funds. Each regional state "Land" is responsible for financing hospital infrastructural investments. However, experience over the last few years revealed that the funds established by states do not even cover the maintenance costs of facilities. Thus, these funds will be insufficient to finance all digital transformation projects in German hospitals. Furthermore, practical experience showed that states implemented their own unofficial preference system for the allocation of funds. In Baden-Württemberg, a state in the south-west part of Germany, the funds are

Table 2 Funding opportunities specified by the Hospital Future Act, based on Klauber et al. (2019)

Minimum standard of digital infrastructure for German hospitals	
1	Establishment of patient portals for digital admission and discharge management, which enable a digital exchange of information between service providers and service recipients as well as between service providers, care or rehabilitation facilities and payers before, during and after treatment in hospitals.
2	Establishment of end-to-end, structured electronic documentation of care and treatment services as well as the establishment of systems that support automated and language-based documentation of care and treatment services.
3	Establishment of partially or fully automated clinical decision support systems that support clinical care providers with the aim of increasing the quality of care in treatment decisions through automated advice and recommendations.
4	Establishment of end-to-end digital medication management to increase drug therapy safety, providing information on all drug-related treatments throughout the entire treatment process in the hospital; these facilities also include robotics-based positioning systems for dispensing medication.
5	Establishment of an internal hospital digital process for requesting services, which enables both the request for services and feedback on the course of treatment of patients in electronic form with the aim of accelerating internal hospital communication processes.
Further areas for funding through the Hospital Future Act	
6	Adaptation of the technical and, in particular, the information technology equipment of the casualty department of hospitals.
7	Measures permissible under competition law necessary to coordinate the range of services offered by several hospitals, to develop a balanced joint service structure that ensures comprehensive care and enables specialization; measures also include the provision of secure systems that make IT infrastructures available via a server network without these being installed on the local server (cloud computing systems).
8	The introduction and further development of an online-based care record system for beds to improve collaboration between hospitals and other care sectors.
9	The procurement, construction, expansion or development of information technology, communications technology and robotics-based equipment, systems or procedures or spatial measures required to support physicians in the treatment of patients, particularly in the context of operations, or to establish telemedicine network structures between hospitals or between hospitals and outpatient facilities and to enable the use of telemedicine procedures for the inpatient care of patients.
10	The procurement, construction, expansion or development of information technology or communications technology equipment, systems, or processes to take appropriate state-of-the-art organizational and technical precautions to prevent disruptions to the availability, integrity, and confidentiality of the hospital operator's information technology systems, components or processes essential to the functionality of the respective hospital and security of the processed patient information.
11	Projects to adapt patient rooms to the special treatment requirements in the event of an epidemic, in particular by converting rooms with more than two beds into single or double-bed rooms, provided that the project results in a corresponding reduction in the number of beds determined by hospital planning.

primarily allocated towards hospital mergers or the closure of hospitals to concentrate the funds and create maximum care providing hospitals.

3.4 Funding on a Micro Level Through Hospitals Own Budget and Contracts with Individual Insurance

The most common way to fund infrastructural digital health transformation projects are the hospitals' own budgets. This is with the help of loans or via internal financing, in which hospitals increase revenues for given operating costs or try to save on personnel and material costs for given revenues. Private hospitals have an advantage, because it is easier for them to acquire funds from the capital market. Furthermore, hospitals are able to arrange contracts with individual health insurance on a project basis. These contracts are designed on a regional or hospital level and include at least one health insurance fund and at least one service provider. In order to create value for all parties involved in these contracts, they focus on the enhancement of healthcare delivery. Furthermore, they mostly aim to reduce the cost for health insurance per insured person in the region or per patient treated in the hospitals. The focus of such contracts is best described by the triple aim approach: improving the quality of care, improving the health of the target population and reducing the per capita cost of healthcare for the health insurance funds.

4 Digital Health Services in Hospitals

In general, hospital services are differentiated according to Section 39 of the German Social Code, Book V (SGB V) into full and partial inpatient services, pre- and post-inpatient services and the area of outpatient operations. Against the backdrop of inpatient remuneration, a distinction is also made between general hospital services and optional services. General hospital services are those services necessary for the medically appropriate and sufficient care of the patient, according to Section 2 (2) BPPflV. Elective services are medical and non-medical forms of treatment that exceed what is medically necessary. The remuneration of elective services is based on a separate contractual agreement between the hospital and the patient. The DRG system (Diagnosis-Related Groups system) according to Section 17b of the German Hospital Financing Act (KHG) forms the basis for the financing of fully and partially inpatient services. Further legal regulations for individual remuneration variants can also be found in the Hospital Remuneration Act (KHEntgG) and in the flat rate per case agreement of the self-governing partners.

The DRG system is a patient classification system and forms the core of the payment system for inpatient services. The procedure that governs the classification is defined. Treatment cases that are medically similar and as homogeneous as possible in terms of their treatment effort are grouped together. The services are then billed to the health insurer on the basis of this allocation, taking into account the billing and coding regulations. Based on certain characteristics, individual inpatient treatment cases, such as a principal and secondary diagnosis or treatment services rendered, etc., can be grouped into case groups.

Within this flat-rate DRG system, the operation and procedure code (OPS) is another important basis for inpatient remuneration. The OPS is the official classification for coding operations, procedures and general medical measures. In this respect, an OPS-coded procedure forms the basis for service billing in the inpatient sector.

In hospitals, the principle of permission with prohibition applies, i.e., in principle, examination and treatment methods (NUB) can be used as long as they have not been excluded by the Federal Joint Committee (G-BA) according to § 137c SGB. In order for hospitals to be allowed to provide innovative services, they must submit an online NUB application to the Institute for the Hospital Remuneration System (InEK) to be reimbursed for them. The system checks whether the service at issue is already included in the DRG catalogue. If this is the case, the service is already reimbursed by the payers. If, on the other hand, the InEK approves the hospital's application, a special charge can be negotiated with the health insurers for the product or procedure. The G-BA can advise hospitals and medical device manufacturers prior to an application as to whether the prerequisites for approval exist. Such a procedure according to §137 h SGB V can be initiated by the first inquiry regarding a new procedure or medical device. It is the task of the G-BA to evaluate the method if the technical application is significantly based on the use of medical devices of high risk classes. In principle, an evaluation by the G-BA is necessary if procedures reveal new theoretical-scientific concepts.

The basis of the evaluation by the G-BA is the benefit of the procedure under review for the patient. If the benefit of the method is considered sufficiently proven, it must be clarified whether quality assurance measures are to be taken. If neither the benefit nor the harmfulness, or the ineffectiveness of the method is considered sufficiently proven, a trial phase is carried out. If, on the other hand, the harmfulness or ineffectiveness of the method is evident, the method is excluded by the G-BA. Reimbursement of these methods is governed by Section 6 (2) KHEntgG for time limited, case-related charges or additional charges.

4.1 *§ 68 a Social Code (SGB) V*

Under Section 68 a of the German Social Code, Book V, health insurance funds were given the opportunity to participate directly in the promotion of digital innovations. Under the Act, they can either participate in a development in cooperation with manufacturers of medical devices, companies from the field of information technology, research institutions, and service providers and communities of service providers, or they can acquire shares in the investment fund. Thus, health insurers have been given the opportunity to promote and finance new innovations together with hospitals.

Examples of advancing digital care in inpatient facilities can be found in many processes. The most prominent are introduced in the following.

5 Funding Through the Innovation Fund

5.1 Optimal@NRW

The project "Optimal@NRW" is supported by the health insurance funds Barmer, DAK, IKK, TK in connection with the Innovation Fund with about 14.9 million Euros for more than 4 years. Opitmal@NRW aims to solve the problems resulting from demographic change with adequate care for geriatric persons. The project designs an intersectoral approach that uses early warning systems, teleconsultation systems and digital treatment documentation to transform the acute care of geriatric persons. A total of 25 nursing homes in the Aachen region, the RWTH Aachen University Hospital and the KV-Nordrhein are directly involved in this project (Cf. G-BA n.d.).

5.2 SeRoDi

In the context of the project "Service robotics for support in person-related services" (SeRoDi), six partners from research and health care have developed three new service robot solutions for inpatient care and analysed their effects on work and service processes. The project promotes use of new technologies in care and thus pursues the goal of relieving care staff and allows more time for actual care activities. The use of modern robot technology in care can relieve the physical strain on care staff and thus prevent long-term illnesses. In addition, people in care can also benefit from service robots, as this promotes and maintains their independence.

Three service robot solutions were developed and tested as part of SeRoDi:

- Multifunctional personal lifter

  The special feature of the personal lift is that it combines the functions of several lifts in one device and has additional assistance functions. It can be ordered by an electronic request from the caregiver where needed. The person lifter is used to assist in lifting persons from the bed, but also in transporting persons in a lying or sitting position. The person to be picked up is automatically recognised by sensors and the lift's pick-up system is positioned accordingly.
- Intelligent nursing trolley

  This is used to support nursing staff through the automated provision of care utensils. After being prompted by smartphone or integrated touchscreens, the intelligent care trolley drives autonomously to the required place of use or follows care staff while they work. The integrated touch screens are also intended for the documentation of material consumption in accordance with legal requirements.

- Service assistant for residents and patients

  The service assistant comes to the resident's or patient's point of stay and brings them the requested items such as drinks, snacks or magazines. The request for delivery is made, for example, by the patient via inpatient multimedia terminals (Cf. SeRoDi Servicerobotik in der Pflege n.d.).

5.3 LAQA SmartCup

The LAQA SmartCup is an intelligent drinking system that reminds the user of fluid intake by light, sound or vibration and automatically records and analyses drinking behaviour. The aim of the project is on the one hand to relieve nursing staff in their daily work by transferring the measured drinking behaviour fully automatically into the drinking protocol or the nursing documentation. The drinking cup can be used in all living environments without any additional effort, as it does not make any technical demands on the environment in which it is used (Cf. LAQA GmbH n.d.).

5.4 Meona

The UKF has also been introducing electronic patient files for several years. For this purpose, the hospital has independently developed the software Meona, which can be used to record vital signs and medicines. In addition, care and treatment steps can be planned and documented, which also facilitates billing. During rounds, the medical staff documents directly in the digital file, which eliminates the need to transfer visit sheets and prevents errors due to illegible writing. The software is also able to compare newly prescribed medication with the patient's age, body weight, possible allergies or elevated kidney values and, if necessary, suggest a different dosage or a suitable alternative medication. In this way, about one third of all medication errors or undesirable side effects can be prevented.

5.5 Evaluation of Microscope Images

In the Department of Ophthalmology at Freiburg University Hospital, microscopic images of the endothelial layer, a wafer-thin layer of cells in the eye, must be viewed regularly. The endothelial cells keep the cornea in the eye transparent by continuously pumping water out of the cornea. However, when the cells die, the cornea becomes cloudy. For this reason, the endothelial cells need to be counted regularly to determine the right time for treatment. For a long time, doctors did the counting by hand, which was both time-consuming and prone to errors. The evaluation is now performed by a self-learning software, which was developed by the eye clinic's team. The software was trained on hundreds of hand-counted images and can now deliver the evaluation of the microscopic images within a few seconds. This gives the doctors time for other activities and reduces the error rate enormously. In addition, the software can be used to examine significantly more images in future studies, making the studies more precise.

5.6 *Mixed Reality in Surgery*

Mixed reality applications offer promising solutions that make surgical planning and performing surgery more precise (Cf. Goyen 2020, p. 26 ff). Mixed reality is a blending of reality with virtual reality. When considering a spectrum from virtual to lived reality, mixed reality is between the two ends of the continuum. Virtual reality in combination with lived reality forms a new world in which the virtual world coexists and interacts with the real world (Cf. Ficarra 2021, p. 97 ff).

One example of a Mixed Reality application in surgery is the VSI Holomedicine by the company ApoQlar from Hamburg. Holomedicine is made up of the terms hologram and medicine and stands for a new type of medical technology in which the real world is augmented by holograms based on real data and appear accordingly as 3D models in physical space (Cf. Pape 2020). The VSI is a mixed reality platform in which CT or MRI images are placed virtually on the operating theatre site through mixed reality glasses, the HoloLens from Microsoft. To use this in surgery, the doctor has to import the image data in DICOM format via drag-and-drop. A 3D object is then automatically generated from these. Furthermore, this can be used in surgery planning, patient education and training (Cf. Medica Magazin 2019).

5.7 *SpeaKlNG*

The self-learning dictation and speech recognition software "SpeaKlNG" supports medical staff in documenting treatments. Findings are dictated and directly processed in writing by speech recognition. The workload for dictations that were previously laboriously typed is reduced to a short final check of the transcription. If manual corrections are made during the final check, the software compares the word and the corrected text. In this way, it constantly expands its vocabulary and can "remember" the user's individual speaking habits and correct them automatically (Cf. Universitätsklinikum Freiburg 2019, p. 32 ff).

5.8 *moio.care-System*

The moio.care system is an intelligent patch consisting of a thin, flexible sensor module barely noticeable on the skin. The patch is applied to the spine and worn by the patient around the clock. An individual profile can be created for each patient via app by activating the various functions of the moio.care system individually and playing them on the sensor.

One function of the system is, for example, a moving signal, which is used in the prevention of pressure sores. The moio.care system detects the patient's movements and identifies them as sufficient positioning movement if there is more than a 30° change in the axis (Cf. Pfannstiel et al. 2020, p. 626 f). Another function of the moio.care system is the patient's positioning. This is particularly useful for patients suffering from dementia (Cf. moio.care n.d.). The function of a stand-up and fall signal ensures increased patient safety (Cf. Pfannstiel et al. 2017, p. 221).

5.9 *Artificial Intelligence in the History and Diagnosis of Breast Cancer*

Breast cancer is the most common type of cancer and the second leading cause of cancer death among women in the world. If breast cancer is detected early, there is a high probability of successful treatment. In order to detect the cancer at an early stage, there are already several standard procedures such as ultrasound, mammography and thermography. These diagnostic images obtained from the examinations have so far been evaluated by the doctors who treat the cancer. Various factors have an influence on the expansion of the images or diagnosis of the disease, which is why different processes have been developed in recent years to support the doctor in the evaluation of the diagnostic images (Cf. Geras et al. (2019).

There are various methods that use AI in the field. One method is **computer-aided diagnosis**. The first CAD system was approved by the Food and Drug Administration (FDA) in 1998. The aim of this method is to help radiologists identify tumours that would not have been detected without AI. The Technology was developed to detect patterns based on supervised machine learning. However, the added clinical benefit behind the method is controversial, because CAD throws up many false-positive results.

DeepMind, Google's AI, is to improve early detection of breast cancer in the future. For this purpose, the artificial intelligence was trained with two data sets of more than 91,000 women in the USA and Great Britain. As a result, the system developed algorithms that recognize the signs of tumour tissue in breast cancer when evaluating diagnostic images. A study was performed involving more than 3000 women from the US and more than 25,000 women from the UK. Mammograms were evaluated once by the AI and then by six radiologists. The AI had significantly better results than the six radiologists. The AI diagnosed 2.7% fewer false negatives in the UK and the error rate in the US was 9.4% lower. For false positives, the CI had a lower error rate of 1.2% and 5.7% in both the UK and the US, respectively (Cf. Urbanek 2020).

Digital medicine in the inpatient sector can be financed within the framework of dual hospital financing, provided that the hospital is included in the state's hospital plan. The prerequisite for this is, for example, that the digital care solution be defined as an investment taken over by the federal states within the framework of the delimitation ordinance. Within this framework, both individual funding and lump-sum funding can be used. However, investments have been declining in recent years. It follows that the hospital will probably have to bear the investment itself and would, therefore, have to consider alternative financing methods, such as internal financing or loan financing.

Another possibility is offered by the Hospital Future Act. According to this, an application for funding would have to be submitted to the state and 30% would then be taken over by the state or hospital operator and 70% would be paid from the three billion euros made available from the health fund. The prerequisite for this, however, is that the state also wants to promote this, since according to the bill there is no entitlement to the funding.

In addition, the hospital can enter into a cooperation agreement with the health insurance funds regarding the financing of digital inpatient care within the framework of Section 68 a of the German Social Code, Book V (SGB V).

The fee in an inpatient care facility is made up as follows (cf. Fig. 4).

In accordance with Section 82 of the German Social Code (SGB) XI, care facilities receive a so-called care allowance, which is used to remunerate general care services as well as a fee for room and board. The care allowance is also known as the care rate. The care allowance is paid by the person in need of care or their cost bearer, while the fee for room and board must be paid by the person in need of care themselves. The amount of the care rate is determined by the care rate agreement concluded between the facility operator and the cost bearers. The performance-related nursing rates are to be evaluated according to uniform principles for all the home's residents. Performance-related means that the nursing rates are adjusted according to the respective degree of nursing care. In addition, the nursing facility

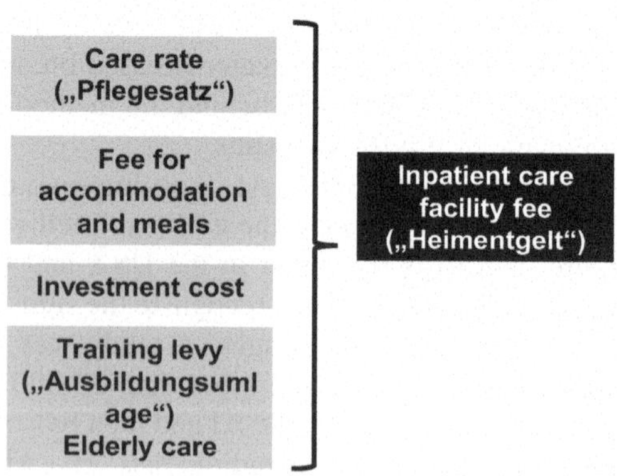

Fig. 4 Part of inpatient care facility fees; own presentation based on Metzger-Gutjahr Stiftung (2022)

is allowed to charge separately for capital expenditures required for operations or for rent, leases, etc. The so-called training levy is intended to equalize the costs of training between facilities that train a lot and facilities that train less. In 2020, the training levy in each full inpatient care facility will be €1.25/day.

6 Take Home

Most German hospitals have missed out on the digital transformation process so far. Major hurdles during the last few years which led to circumstances of lack of adequate funding, missing qualified IT-personnel and hospital management's willingness for change. The legislator is now trying to gradually introduce incentives for the introduction of digital services, e.g. through additional funding as part of the hospital future act. In addition, hospital management is required to develop a strategy to be able to attain a minimum digitization standard. The authors of this chapter are convinced that the time could not be better for a digital service provider to enter the German market. On the one hand the additional funding opportunities enhance the possibilities for implementation of digitalization projects. On the other hand hospitals are forced to adapt to the rapidly changing environment to be able to stay competitive. We will see a diminishing number of hospitals in Germany but also experience a rapidly increasing level of digitalization and thus ultimately better care for patients.

References

Ficarra, Barbara. (2021) Virtual Reality, Mixed Reality and Augmented Reality. 2021; in Whende, Carroll: Emerging Technologies for nurses), S. 95–126.

G-BA (n.d.): https://innovationsfonds.g-ba.de/projekte/neue-versorgungsformen/optimalatnrw-optimierte-akutversorgung-geriatrischer-patienten-durchein-intersektorales-telemedizinisches-koopertionsnetzwerk-rund-um-die-uhr.364; last accessed January 24 2022

Geras, K., Mann, R., Moy, L. (2019) Artificial Intelligence for Mammography and Digital Breast Tomosynthesis: Current Concepts and Future Perspectives, Radiology, 293, 2, 246–259.

Goyen, Mathias (2020): Digitalisierung der Medizintechnik zur Verbesserung der Patientenversorgung in der EU, in Baas, Jens: Digitale Gesundheit in Europa, Berlin, S. 26–35.

Klauber, J., Geraedts, M., Friedrich, J. & Wasem, J. 2019. *Krankenhaus-Report 2019: Das digitale Krankenhaus*, Springer Nature.

LAQA GmbH (n.d.) Drinking made smart: https://l-aqa.de/, last accessed January 24 2022

Loos, S., Albrecht, M. & Zich, K. 2019. *Zukunftsfähige Krankenhausversorgung: Simulation und Analyse einer Neustrukturierung der Krankenhausversorgung am Beispiel einer Versorgungsregion in Nordrhein-Westfalen* [Online]. Bertelsmann Stiftung. Available: https://www.bertelsmann-stiftung.de/fileadmin/files/BSt/Publikationen/GrauePublikationen/VV_Bericht_KH-Landschaft_final.pdf [Accessed 24.01.2021].

Medica Magazin (2019): Virtual Surgery Intelligence: mit der Microsoft Hololens im OP, https://www.medica.de/de/News/Interviews/%C3%84ltere_Interviews/Interviews_2019/Virtual_Surgical_Intelligence_mit_der_Microsoft_Hololens_im_OP, last accessed January 24 2022

Metzger-Gutjahr Stiftung. (2022). *Zusammensetzung Heimentgelt* (o.J.); http://http://metzger-gutjahr.de/stationaerepflege/zusammensetzung-der-heimkosten/. Accessed 24 Jan 2022

moio.care (n.d.): Das moio.care System; https:moio.care/das-moio/, last accessed January 24 2022

Pape, Katrin (2020): Holomedizin: Erste Herz-Operation unter Mixed-Reality-Technologie, https://www.aspekteins.com/holomedizin-erste-herzoperation-unter-mixed-reality-technologie/, last accessed January 24 2022.

Pfannstiel, Mario A., Kassel, Kristin, Rasche, Christoph (2020): Innovationen und Innovationsmanagement im Gesundheitswesen, Technologien, Produkte und Dienstleistungen voranbringen. Springer, Wiesbaden

Pfannstiel, Mario A., Jaeckel, Roger, Da-Cruz Patrick (2020): Market Access im Gesundheitswesen, Hürden und Zugangswege zur Gesundheitsversorgung, Wiesbaden

Pfannstiel, Mario A., Da-Cruz, Patrick, Mehlich, Harald (2017): Digitale Transformation von Dienstleistungen im Gesundheitswesen II; Impulse für das Management; Springer, Wiesbaden

SeRoDi Servicerobotik in der Pflege (n.d.); Über SeRoDi: https://www.serodi.de/, last accessed January 24 2022

Universitätsklinikum Freiburg (2019): Das Magazin - Digitale Medizin, Ausgabe 03/2019; https://www.uniklinikfreiburg.de/fileadmin/mediapool/06_presse/pdfs-publikationen/dasmagazin/2019/UKF_DasMagazin_3_2019.pdf last accessed January 24 2022

Urbanek (2020): Wer Brustkrebs besser diagnostiziert, URL: https://www.aerztezeitung.de/Wirtschaft/Wer-Brustkrebs-besser-diagnostiziert-405409.html. Last accessed January 24 2022

Digitalization of Nursing to Overcome Staffing Shortages? Categorization and Market Access of Digital Applications

Jan-Marc Hodek

1 Introduction: Will Robots Lead to a Nursing Workforce Without Humans?

In many industries, digitized processes have long been a part of normal routine. More and more, processes are being standardized and automated with the help of digital solutions. The question is whether this trend will also revolutionize the healthcare sector. The German healthcare system is still in the early stages of this change. In most public discussions, it is the claims rather than the opportunities of new technologies that are emphasized (McKinsey & Company 2018).

The aim of this article is to highlight the possibility of greater digitalization of nursing and long-term care. Even if nursing and long-term care might at first glance seem unsuitable candidates for the mentioned trends toward standardization and automation, it is worth taking a closer look at the aspects of nursing that are well suited to stronger digital support.

We chat with our friends on our smartphones; we can find our way in new surroundings while on the move thanks to Google Maps; and fitness trackers on our wrists accompany us in daily life. In contrast, everyday work in nursing remains comparatively unaffected by digitalization. However, the digital change will also impact nursing and long-term care. All players in the market—statutory health insurance providers, compulsory long-term care providers, outpatient and inpatient service providers and, above all, patients and their relatives—will soon find themselves in a completely different world of care (Merda et al. 2017).

According to the Federal Statistical Office, there are around 1.1 million nurses in Germany (including emergency service nurses and midwives). In addition, there are almost 650,000 elderly-care nurses. Nursing staff thus represent the largest

J.-M. Hodek (✉)
RWU – Ravensburg-Weingarten University of Applied Sciences, Weingarten, Germany
e-mail: hodek@rwu.de

S. Walzer (ed.), *Digital Healthcare in Germany*, Contributions to Economics,
https://doi.org/10.1007/978-3-030-94025-6_6

professional group in the German healthcare system. However, although the number of nurses has increased in recent years, it will probably not be enough to meet the future growth in demand. According to studies, the number of people in need of care will increase from around four million today to more than five million by 2040. Because more and more baby boomers (including those who work as nurses themselves) are retiring at the same time, it is obvious that a solution cannot be achieved by more and more skilled personnel alone. According to estimates, Germany already has a shortage of several tens of thousands of skilled nurses. The lack of nursing staff is becoming increasingly apparent in hospitals, retirement homes, and ambulatory care services. The result is high work intensity and lack of time for caregivers (Statistisches Bundesamt 2019; Statistisches Bundesamt 2020; Fachinger and Mähs 2019).

Digitalization and robotics constitute possible solutions to overcome the shortage of skilled workers. The aim is to enable elderly people to be cared for at home for as long as possible. It should be noted that a large number of technical aids are already used to provide support today. Without these aids, far more human nursing staff would already be needed.

Digitalization and new technologies offer the opportunity to leverage efficiency potential. They provide hope of managing with fewer staff and/or of lowering costs while maintaining at least the same (or possibly even higher) quality of care.

The aim is to relieve overstretched staff of bureaucracy and care-related side activities (such as food delivery or laundry transport) in order to use the time regained in real care work close to the patient. The potential of digital technologies is seen above all in the areas of documentation, information processing, organization, and communication among nursing staff (Fachinger and Mähs 2019; McKinsey & Company 2018).

2 Fears and Hopes

Irrespective of whether we regard it with anxiety or hope that the storm will pass, the digitalization of all areas of life is sure to come to pass. Even data protection concerns and "German Angst" will not change the situation. History teaches us that the technical possibilities that simply make our lives easier will always prevail. It is important to emphasize that change is not just a threat but can also be an opportunity: It always benefits those market participants who do not allow themselves to become too comfortable in their established position and accept the change. The situation is no different with the digitalization of the healthcare system.

In this way, nursing staff and their employers can also benefit from this change and perhaps even be more successful than ever. Fears of job losses and care with no human touch, which is particularly widespread among nurses, can be countered with some hopes.

Nursing is facing major challenges due to pressure from two sides:

- a reduction in the provision of care due to the shortage of skilled workers (fewer care workers in cohorts with comparatively low birth rates), yet at the same time
- more demand for care due to demographic changes in society.

Robotics and digitalization can therefore be of great help in maintaining or even improving quality of care.

3 An Attempt to Categorize

One opportunity presented by digitalization lies is the possibility of increasing work productivity. This could relieve nursing staff of administrative tasks, heavy physical work, or (unskilled) ancillary activities, thus enabling them to devote more time to the actual core tasks of nursing. Technology can help older people to live independently at home for longer. The various ideas are so diverse that they need to be categorized (Merda et al. 2017; Fachinger and Mähs 2019; Hodek 2020):

3.1 Logistics for Food, Materials, Laundry, Medications, and Laboratory Results

- Service robotics: These robots work in direct contact with the patient or resident. Like a digital butler, providers such as Care-O-bot or Pepper can provide food and drinks, deliver magazines to the patient's bed, or provide entertainment (games and music). Cleaning robots can also be counted in this group.
- Transportation robotics: This category includes devices for (automatic) bed transport. It also includes deliveries of laundry directly to the patient's bed, as well as the automated supply of sterile surgical kits and portioning and delivery of pharmaceuticals.

3.2 Emotional Robotics: Entertainment and Interaction Offers

This category includes, for example, the cuddly seal called Paro. Even though everyone knows these stuffed animals are not actually alive, some studies show that this type of robotics is well received by those in need of care. These socially interactive robots can interact directly with patients and care-home residents. They can react to gestures and facial expressions and sometimes show such expressions themselves. Specific applications include speaking to, entertaining, or calming down people with dementia.

3.3 Technical Aids to Relieve the Physical Strain on Caregivers

This category consists of robotic arms, exoskeletons, and mobile or permanently installed training devices at the patient's bed; special mattresses for prophylaxis of decubitus; special turning/lifting devices for obese patients; and much more. The objective is to support nursing staff with higher safety standards and to relieve them from the exhausting mobilization and repositioning of patients.

One example, from the field of rehabilitation, is the mobilization of stroke patients. Currently, patient-specific rehabilitation exercises are carried out manually by physiotherapists or nursing staff. In the future, these physically demanding and time-consuming tasks could be carried out automatically by technical helpers. Initially, the human expert would teach the patient how to use the robot assistant for their rehabilitation exercises, and the robot would then repeat the very same exercises in subsequent sessions. In addition to the advantage of freeing up staff time, this would increase the patient's independence, enabling them to perform their exercises whenever and wherever it suits them.

3.4 Technical Support from Background Systems, e.g. for Administrative Tasks

Examples are electronic documentation; planning of patient appointments and visits based on artificial intelligence; and voice-activated assistants. The routine assessments that are frequently required to determine the individual care needs of patients can also be digitized. This also includes information on accompanying inpatient admissions. Especially in this field of computer-assisted documentation, surveys among nursing staff show that digital solutions are already widespread: Approximately 80% of nurses in inpatient elderly care and around 70% in hospitals state that they already use this type of digitalization as a part of their everyday work. Ideally, this should save staff save time and walking distance, enable them to document more quickly, and result in fewer mistakes.

3.5 Telemonitoring/Telecare

The aim of this remote monitoring is usually to bridge the physical distance between patient and carer. This digitalization category includes, for example, ambient assisted-living systems with fall sensors and alarm functions or automatic monitoring of vital data and position data (for personal location). In addition to wearables such as watches with fall sensors, sensor modules that are worn on the skin or special flooring systems in old people's homes can be used. This category also includes drug dispensers for better adherence to medication dosage schedules. Doctors or nurses can enter the dosage plan digitally, and the device then reminds the patient to take the medication at the set time by means of an acoustic signal and issues the correct dose at the push of a button.

3.6 Nursing in a Narrower Sense

This refers to nursing procedures such as washing patients or changing bandages, etc. The current generation of robots, however, is still a long way from providing these core nursing services in a manner than is even halfway acceptable. Nevertheless, initial ideas and research projects are underway, such as:

- the "Robotic Nurse Assistant Cody" from the Georgia Institute of Technology (USA), who in the distant future could wash patients independently or accompany them while they walk around,
- washing systems for people, and
- automatic feeding arms for people with severe mobility impairments (for example the meal assistance robot called "My Spoon" from a Japanese provider).

These systems do exist as marketable offers, but are currently still a long way from being widely used in the German healthcare system.

3.7 Digital Nursing Applications (DiPA)

These apps are specifically tailored to the nursing sector. Several of the categories mentioned above—such as telemonitoring of people in need of care, interactive offers, documentation of (medical-care-related) information, or digital assistance in the broadest sense—could be integrated into these apps. The entire nursing process can also be monitored on an app via a kind of control center. This area will be examined in more detail in the following. Could nursing soon take place by app and smartphone?

4 Nursing Via App and Smartphone? Digital Health Applications

4.1 Overview

Health insurance providers in Germany are seeing an increasing demand for "digital health applications" (DiGA), which have recently become prescribable and reimbursable. In addition to these DiGA, "digital care applications" specifically designed to support nursing (called DiPA for short) will soon be eligible for prescription. Germany is thus the first country worldwide in which regular reimbursement for digital healthcare applications is possible. The specific approval and reimbursement processes for DiPA will be closely aligned with the processes already established for DiGA.

DiGA and DiPA include apps and web-based applications. Their main function is to create a positive health outcome for patients. This outcome is an important prerequisite for inclusion in the official register of the German Federal Institute for Drugs and Medical Devices (BfArM).

At the moment, the official listing and thus prescribability of digital apps specifically for the nursing sector is at a very early stage. However, some suitable applications can already be found in the app stores. These could possibly find their way into the reimbursement catalog in the future.

4.2 Digital Nursing Applications Outside the Official Listing

The various app stores contain numerous offerings available to self-payers in the area of digital care/digital nursing support. They cover a broad range of activities and show how varied digital health support can be in the area of nursing. However, statements about proof of benefit and certificates for (data) security are so far comparatively underdeveloped. Examples of these applications include:

- Offers for seniors who want to improve their mobility through exercises. This also includes therapy offers to strengthen cognitive and communicative skills and game-based assistance technologies for mobility training. (Auto)biography work as well as learning and memory games can be integrated into this offering.
- Interactive online nursing courses, which help relatives and volunteers to prepare for providing home care and enable the person in need of care to live a self-determined life for as long as possible.
- Offers to support care-giving relatives and volunteers in their daily care (learning videos for correct handling and use of care aids, tips for care-friendly living, assistance in calculating financial support, etc.).
- Support in finding suitable service providers: contact details for outpatient care services, escort and visiting services, meals-on-wheels providers, doctors, assisted-living facilities, or inpatient care facilities.
- Relatives' apps that provide a live connection to a recipient's home in cases of emergency, complemented by a motion profile or wearables with fall sensors (as a replacement for a conventional home emergency call system).

4.3 *Outlook: Official Reimbursement Process for Digital Care Applications (DiPA)*

Digital care offerings can support nursing provided by professional nursing staff or family caregivers. Similar to the field of DiGA, the BfArM will in future also be responsible for approving and testing digital applications in this nursing area. Only apps listed in the register are actually prescribable and thus reimbursable by the insurance provider. However, these digital care/nursing applications will then be reimbursed by the compulsory long-term care insurance provider (not by the health insurance provider). This insurance provider decides on the necessity of a nursing application. According to the legislator, digital care applications are software- or web-based care offerings that

- help the person in need of care themselves or
- are used during interactions with relatives and professional caregivers.

The aim is to maintain the independence of the person in need of care. Applications of this type can be used for organizing and handling everyday care, or for special care situations, such as maintaining mobility or managing dementia. This also includes applications that are primarily used by family caregivers. Importantly, if the use of the digital application requires additional nursing support services—for example, accompanying the insured person in the specific digital care situation—these can be reimbursed as well.

Again, the German BfArM will be given responsibility for developing a procedure to assess the reimbursability of a DiPA. The procedure will be two-pronged, in alignment with the DiGA procedure, to allow either permanent or provisional inclusion of a DiPA in the register. A very important point is the distinction between lifestyle products and "real nursing". It is not the task of long-term care insurance providers to finance applications such as smart home products or everyday objects such as fitness trackers.

What are the criteria for measuring a significant health benefit, and how could this benefit be evaluated? Aspects such as strengthening the self-determination or participation of the person in need of care must be operationalized for this purpose. Endpoints could be the regaining of independence and abilities in various areas of daily life. The established measure of health-related quality of life could also serve as means of evaluating benefits.

Similar to DiGA, the following applies to negotiating a specific reimbursement price: The manufacturer of a digital care application negotiates the price of a DiPA with the central association of the long-term care insurance provider (after the digital care application has been included in the register). The criteria to be assessed include aspects such as security and technical functionality, as well as data protection and, above all, the benefits to nursing outcomes (Bundesregierung 2020).

What is the appropriate price? The same evidence requirements that apply to other services paid by the insurance provider must also apply to DiPA. In the future, it is conceivable that—similar to the German reference price system for pharmaceuticals—maximum amounts for groups of comparable applications could also be set for DiGA and DiPA.

5 Market Access and Reimbursement: Costs and Benefits

Nursing robots are currently associated with very high-cost investments; this is very similar to the situation for industrial robots. However, if the volume of production increases in the next few years, prices could fall significantly (similar to the computer industry), and thus the degree of market penetration would increase. Compared with the costs of human labor, robotic labor is likely to be less expensive in the long term. There are some basic cost–benefit considerations to be made here:

- On the one hand, robots are initially associated with high acquisition costs (plus energy, maintenance, and repair costs). If you are already considering purchasing, you can expect prices up to the six-digit range.
- On the other hand, there is no regular salary to pay. The robot does not take vacations and does not get sick; there are no social insurance contributions; and the device can work far more than the 8 h per day that are worked by most humans. Nor is he aware of weekends or public holidays. His resistance to stress is better, and failure due to tiredness disappears. Thanks to software updates, he can always be up to date with the latest knowledge.

In summary, digital solutions and nursing robotics could help to lighten the load of human care workers. Presumably this will make it possible to cope with the great challenges of future care provision in the first place. The human nursing staff could increasingly devote themselves to the actual core task of caring for people.

By performing routine tasks (such as service activities, transport, or electronic documentation), robotic assistance systems can ensure that caregivers are now spared some (frustrating) work steps.

However, it is also important to be aware that the integration of digital applications (no matter what kind) into the standard care of the primary healthcare market, including financing through health insurance, requires serious proof of benefit. For this benefit assessment of innovative digital applications, a standardized procedure similar to, but adapted from, that used to assess pharmaceuticals is required (Elmer 2017). High-quality evidence-based studies of the benefits (and costs) of digital nursing offers are far too few to date.

6 Conclusions

In Germany, the digitalization of the healthcare system is less advanced overall than in other regions of the world, such as Scandinavia or North America. Effectiveness potential has so far been underutilized (McKinsey & Company 2018). The fields of application primarily concern organizational matters in the background of nursing, some peripheral areas such as transport and logistics issues, and the support of the person in need of care by means of apps. However, nursing robots will not (yet) be able to completely replace humans as caregivers in the foreseeable future.

Nonetheless, the opportunities of digitalization are now known to almost all those involved in the healthcare system—including those in nursing. Companies, organizations, and end consumers (i.e. people in need of care and their relatives) all need a reliable legal framework and possibly also public (financial) support (Elmer 2017). A major contribution can already be made today to counteract the shortage of nursing staff. In the long term, it is a matter of ensuring qualitatively appropriate nursing through technical/digital support. Above all, robots will probably gradually be able to perform non-care service activities as well as (unskilled) ancillary activities. There is also hope that the physical and mental health of today's overburdened caregivers and relatives will improve as a result of this alleviation from certain tasks. In particular, some time-consuming and physically demanding routine activities could soon be taken over by robots or other digital applications. This will not lead to a substitution of skilled nurses but will give precisely these skilled workers more time for direct interaction with those in need of care (Fachinger and Mähs 2019).

For this to be possible, digital applications in nursing must be subject to the same safety rules, proof of benefits, and cost-effectiveness standards as any other innovation in our healthcare system. Firstly, this serves to protect patients and, secondly, protects the financiers of the health system from having to co-finance uneconomical approaches perhaps only because they are currently in vogue. In a nutshell: If a digital solution or a robot is useful and economical (from an evidence-based point of view), then it should be purchased. In nursing, too, efficiency means getting the best possible care out of scarce financial and human resources. Digitalization can make a contribution to this.

Sources

Bundesregierung (2020): Referentenentwurf des Bundesministeriums für Gesundheit – Entwurf eines Gesetzes zur digitalen Modernisierung von Versorgung und Pflege (Digitale Versorgung und Pflege - Modernisierungs-Gesetz – DVPMG) (date: 15.11.2020).

Elmer, A. (2017): Die Digitalisierung des Gesundheitswesens – Handlungsempfehlungen für Politik und Akteure, in: GGW, 17, Issue 3, pp. 23–30.

Fachinger, U., Mähs, M. (2019): Digitalisierung und Pflege, in: Klauber, J. et al. (Hrsg.): Krankenhausreport 2019, pp. 115–128.

Hodek, J.M. (2020): Das deutsche Gesundheitssystem für Dummies, 1. Auflage, Wiley-VCH Verlag, Weinheim.

McKinsey & Company (2018): Digitalisierung in deutschen Krankenhäusern – Eine Chance mit Milliardenpotenzial für das Gesundheitssystem, URL: https://www.mckinsey.de/publikationen/digitalisierung-chance-mit-milliardenpotenzial (date 20.12.2020).
Merda, M., Schmidt, K., Kähler, B. (2017): Pflege 4.0 – Einsatz moderner Technologien aus der Sicht professionell Pflegender, Forschungsbericht, Berufsgenossenschaft für Gesundheitsdienst und Wohlfahrtspflege, BGWforschung, Hamburg.
Statistisches Bundesamt (2019): Statistisches Jahrbuch 2019 – Kapitel 4 Gesundheit, Wiesbaden.
Statistisches Bundesamt (2020): Pflegestatistik 2019 – Pflege im Rahmen der Pflegeversicherung, Deutschlandergebnisse, Wiesbaden.

Reimbursement and Pricing

Stefan Walzer, Roman Spelsberg, and Lutz Vollmer

The achievable price always plays a central role—also for digital health applications as, multiplied by the sales volume—it determines achievable sales revenues and thus the company's income.

In principle, the price for a digital health solution can first be set on the basis of the costs incurred in producing the service. This is particularly relevant for companies that want to be the cost leader for their product and create added value solely by comparing costs with the reference price. Secondly, pricing can be oriented towards the value of the added value created. This so-called value-based pricing is usually more desirable from a company's perspective and might also be associated with quality leadership or niche specialization. Thirdly, strategic considerations of the company can flow into the pricing, regardless of cost savings or benefits gained from the respective service. For example, a price can be chosen below the manufacturing costs at market entry to deter competitors from entering the market on the one hand and to make a profit at a later point in time due to the high unit numbers on the other hand. The most prominent example might be Amazon in various business areas.

Depending on the market segment, the achievable price can be very different. The more customers (segments) one wants to reach with the DiGA, the lower the achievable price usually is. The optimal price, therefore, also depends on the number of units that can be realized with it. Furthermore, price comparators or socalled price

S. Walzer (✉)
MArS Market Access & Pricing Strategy GmbH, Weil am Rhein, Germany

State University Baden-Wuerttemberg, Lörrach, Germany

RWU – Ravensburg-Weingarten University of Applied Sciences, Weingarten, Germany
e-mail: Stefan.walzer@marketaccess-pricingstrategy.de

R. Spelsberg · L. Vollmer
MArS Market Access & Pricing Strategy GmbH, Weil am Rhein, Germany
e-mail: roman.spelsberg@marketaccess-pricingstrategy.de;
lutz.vollmer@marketaccess-pricingstrategy.de

S. Walzer (ed.), *Digital Healthcare in Germany*, Contributions to Economics,
https://doi.org/10.1007/978-3-030-94025-6_7

anchors are taken into account here insofar as added value or cost savings are always analyzed in comparison to competitors and their prices.

Health economic evaluation offers a structured method to determine both savings and value-based prices for the healthcare system which are generally based on three central and successive categories of economic evaluation. These are the costing of individual services, the modelling of care pathways and associated total costs and finally, the synthesis of all the information on the costs and effects of a service in the form of a cost-effectiveness estimate.

Pricing in the SHI is initially cost-based. If a digital health service is included in the reimbursement catalogue, the expenditure associated with the service is calculated to determine the reimbursement. Such a reimbursement could (theoretically) be linked to the development and production cost of a new service. However, the pricing of an innovation is often based on whether and how high cost savings can be achieved by applying the innovation compared to the reimbursement of current care. For this purpose, an entire care process with all the individual services contained therein may have to be mapped in a mathematical model, which represents a central step in the implementation of economic evaluations. Value-based pricing is of great importance, especially for new digital health services with (to be) proven additional benefits. It might be carried out for price negotiations, in special cases on the basis of an economic evaluation. Value-based decision-making represents the ideal type of use of health economic evaluations, in which all the evidence justifying the value proposition (both on costs and health benefits) is quantitatively summarised in a calculation and usually expressed as a cost-effectiveness ratio. The chapter gives a brief supplementary introduction to economic evaluation and refers to further literature. Finally, strategic aspects independent of the direct added value of a service also play an important role in pricing in the healthcare system.

1 Pricing for Digital Health Solutions

1.1 Cost-Based Pricing

Regardless of the market situation for a new digital health application, the absolute long-term price floor must first be determined from the company's point of view. It results from the so-called cost price. In planning, it must be taken into account that a value-based surcharge for the DiGA may not be possible (e.g. in a market with many competitors or with an already available maximum reimbursement amount). In such a scenario, profitable maintenance of the DiGA can only be attained by optimizing the cost structure. In this case, operational costs can be saved in production (e.g. by means of optimized development cost for newer versions of the DiGA) or in sales (e.g. optimization of marketing expenses, sales force optimization, etc.) and profits can be increased accordingly even with constant sales.

1.2 Value-Based Pricing

Value-based pricing means that the price of a good is based on the value of the good to the customer. From an economic perspective, this is the reference model for ideal pricing. The amount of added value is expressed in the customer's maximum willingness to pay for the good. The (added) value created by the company is defined as the difference between the maximum willingness to pay and the (long-term) unit costs.

In principle, patients can also be imagined as customers, especially for digital health and thus be understood as consumers who privately demand healthcare goods. In addition, individual health insurance funds or the SHI system as a whole can be relevant customers if digital health goods are directly reimbursed, e.g. in the case of new DiGA with proven additional benefits. It is true that these must ultimately orient themselves to the added value for end customers of the first (SHI) and second (private demand) healthcare market. However, depending on the importance of these two end customers for their own sales, their own cost position or their own preferences, they may be able to bring additional individual dimensions of added value into the purchase decision and, for example, be prepared to pay a premium for a device with an especially elegant design or colour scheme in the style of the practice rooms or with particular user-friendliness.

Pricing determines which share of this created value remains with the company itself (the so-called "producer surplus")—i.e. increases profits in the form of a surcharge. The other part of the value is left with the customer (the so-called "consumer surplus")—in most cases customers would have bought a product even if it had cost a little more. The difference between the maximum willingness to pay and the market price is, therefore, the customers' "profit" (Fig. 1).

When skimming off a higher price compared to an existing product, it remains to be noted that the assumed added value of a product can be assessed differently by a company than by the buyer of the product, and that buyers only have a limited interest in revealing their maximum willingness to pay or in paying the maximum price. In the case of an anonymous mass market, this leads to a price-sales function: the producer must choose a sales price based on the presumed behaviour of customers, and depending on its level, more or fewer customers demand the product. In

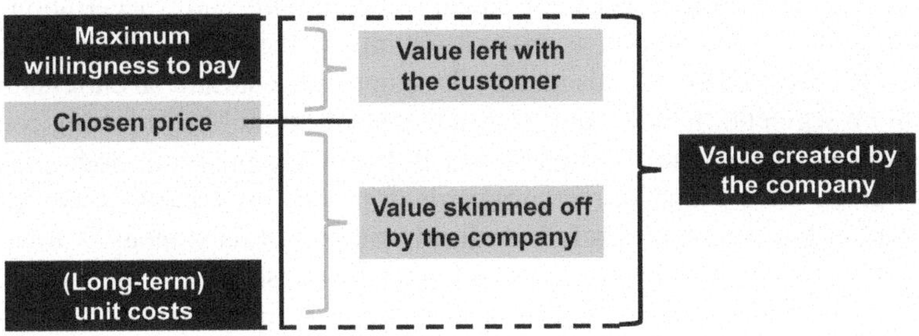

Fig. 1 Exemplary representation of consumer and producer surplus

Fig. 2 Graphical representation of a negotiated solution. Source: Own representation based on Gregson et al. (2005)

the case of a market with little demand (e.g. in the case of individually created products or services), this is expressed in negotiations with different buyer and seller price expectations. Price negotiations therefore move within a bandwidth, the upper end of which represents the customers' maximum willingness to pay. The lower end is represented by the company's long-term unit costs (a service can only be provided if the price is higher than the costs) as well as, if applicable, the financing conditions and different market conditions (competition, influence on other markets, etc.). The negotiated price is in the area of tension between the internal requirements for a return on investment (ROI) and prices that can be achieved on the market (Fig. 2).

Value-based pricing is often associated with the attempt to differentiate buyers according to their willingness to pay. This would mean that the same (or a very similar) product can be sold at higher prices to customers with a higher willingness to pay. Ideally (from the manufacturer's point of view), prices can be negotiated individually with customers. However, in the German DiGA context a company would likely need to decide beforehand whether they want to focus on the SHI or the patient individual market.

1.3 Strategic Considerations in Pricing

Regardless of the size of the added value, further strategic considerations should be taken into account with respect to pricing. For the dynamic perspective, for example, a distinction can be made between so-called skimming and "penetration". In a skimming strategy, an attempt is made to skim off the high willingness to pay, which can lead to a quick amortisation of development costs and an entrenchment in the premium segment. In the medium term, there is the possibility of using consumer discrimination to serve the willingness to pay below the premium price. Examples would be new, more powerful memory cards or processors initially very expensive on the market but whose prices fall. A disadvantage of this strategy is lower sales volumes at market launch and associated higher unit costs. In the digital healthcare market, the skimming strategy could be considered in the context of patient individualized health apps with add-on features.

A penetration strategy tends to be used to quickly gain market share in a highly competitive market with the lowest possible price for the market launch, on the one hand, and to set the highest possible market entry barrier for possible new competitors on the other. The penetration strategy can also be combined in a slightly modified form with various possibilities for price differentiation (e.g. via discounts to end customers such as hospitals, sale of product bundles, etc.). A fundamental disadvantage of the penetration strategy is the risk to one's own brand, as it may be associated as a "cheap product" with poor quality.

1.4 Privately Paid (Premium) Price

The individual willingness to pay is also decisive for the purchase decision for some of the "classic" health services according to the delimitation of the health expenditure account. Thus, some services, especially in the outpatient sector, are generally not reimbursable or have been excluded from the benefits catalogue. Digital health applications have mainly been sold in the privately paid market before the introduction of the so-called DiGA law in 2020.

In addition, willingness to pay also plays a role in the demand for digital services with co-payments and for prices above the so-called reference prices.

From the point of view of a digital health company, a fundamental advantage of the strategy of positioning a new service to patients directly, is that such a market offer can be implemented comparatively quickly and that potentially high premium prices can also be achieved. However, it must be taken into account that in this area only very low sales volumes are generally achieved in Germany. This is mainly due to the fundamentally low willingness to pay of patients in Germany, who consider healthcare goods to be goods that the insurance system has to finance.

1.5 Pricing in the SHI and Economic Evaluation

In analogy to pricing in the secondary healthcare market, four categories can also be distinguished to price a new service in statutory health insurance in Germany:

- Cost-based surcharge when setting new reimbursement rates
- No extra charge: savings in existing supply
- Value-based surcharge for new digital health solutions according to the DiGA law
- Strategic considerations in pricing

However, since it is a matter of using scarce resources for public tasks, criteria other than individual willingness to pay in connection with the interplay of supply and demand on markets are decisive. This is also expressed, among other things, in the application of methods of health economic evaluation in the price determination for new services in the healthcare system.

1.6 Cost-Based Surcharge

In principle, the SHI is oriented towards cost-based pricing: new services that meet the criteria of positive reimbursement decisions are to be reimbursed for the amount of their costs incurred in the healthcare operation. Based on this understanding, willingness to pay is not differentiated from the costs of the service from the perspective of the service provider in the SHI, which also includes the costs of the new digital health service.

The costs of a medical service are understood to be the value of all resources consumed in the production of the service. The business calculation of the total costs of a service unit (socalled full cost accounting in contrast to “partial cost accounting”, which only takes selected costs into account) is usually divided into three stages (Cf. Frod 2011, p. 55ff; Keun and Prott 2009, p. 158ff):

- Cost-type accounting answers the question of which costs have been incurred. All costs are initially taken from the accounting system and recorded according to their type. This includes in particular, capital commitment costs, costs for insurance and contributions (e.g. contributions to the medical association, medical liability insurance), storage costs (e.g. costs for storing medical consumables), costs for administrative and laboratory supplies (e.g. medicines, treatment materials, laboratory materials), general operating costs (e.g. costs for the medical service). Medicines, treatment materials, laboratory materials), general operating costs (e.g. telephone, waiting room equipment), personnel costs (e.g. salaries, training allowances), room costs (e.g. rent, cleaning, maintenance), travel and further training costs (e.g. further training materials, accommodation costs) and equipment costs (e.g. acquisition and maintenance of medical equipment).
- Cost centre accounting answers the question of where the costs were incurred. These costs are assigned to the organizational areas in which they were incurred or in which they can most likely be influenced. These can be departments of a hospital, for example. Not all costs can be assigned directly. These so-called overhead costs (e.g. rent or property tax for the entire building complex) must be allocated to the cost centres with suitable distribution keys (e.g. area of the respective units).
- Cost unit accounting determines which costs have been incurred for what and by what amount. The costs incurred are finally allocated to the units of service provided to be able to compare the costs of service provision with the price achieved. Cost units can be individual services rendered; for inpatient care, DRG-reimbursed cases represent central cost units. Whereas direct costs can be directly allocated to cost units, overhead costs are usually allocated using the distribution keys developed in cost centre accounting.

How exactly the costs of services are collected and transformed into a remuneration level differs between outpatient and inpatient care in the same way as for reimbursement and for the assumption of services. Basically, both reimbursement schemes are oriented towards full cost accounting, whereby in the inpatient sector, due to the responsibility of the Länder for investments, only current care costs are mapped.

1.7 No Extra Charge: Savings in Existing Supply

In many cases, the development of a new remuneration figure with a cost-based surcharge that includes the additional costs of the good offered by one's own company is either not possible for companies or cannot be implemented within a time horizon acceptable for the company. The question then arises whether the costs for the new digital health good can be compensated by savings elsewhere, so that the company's business case can be based on cost-neutral additional benefits or even added value in the form of additional benefits and savings.

It is important to include the issue of perspective when considering costs—costs of a health service can be incurred by very different actors in the health system in different amounts, and accordingly looking at costs from the perspective of only one service provider can give a very incomplete picture. For example, a GP might spend more time on thorough digital respiratory education as part of an improved care process for the care of a COPD patient. This subsequently reduces the number of costly exacerbations, so that the additional costs at the GP are partially offset or even result in overall savings. Such cost effects are not included in the consideration solely from the perspective of individual service providers.

Perspective is an important aspect of health economic cost analyses. A distinction can be made between costs from the perspective of individual service providers or the SHI system as a whole; costs from the perspective of other sectors (e.g. care costs borne by long-term care insurance), costs from the perspective of the patient and his family (e.g. travel costs to the doctor) and costs from the societal perspective, which also includes so-called indirect costs (Cf. Drummond 2005, p. 18ff) productivity losses due to incapacity to work, disability and premature death.

According to these different perspectives, a company can verify with whom savings are most likely to be expected and who is accordingly most likely to be willing to pay as a customer for the new health good—which is not always the service provider itself (for example, in the example of the digital care process for COPD patients mentioned above).

There are three steps to be taken when determining costs in health economic evaluations (Cf. Krauth et al. 2005):

1. Identification of the required use of resources,
2. Quantity recording of resource consumption and
3. Evaluation of the resources used.

An analysis of the added value of medical innovations solely on the basis of associated cost savings bears the name of cost-minimisation analysis in the health economic evaluation literature. In this, it is assumed that the benefits of the different alternatives are equal, so that analysis of the benefits can focus on costs alone. In this form of analysis, therefore, all care costs with the intervention under study are calculated and compared with the costs of relevant comparative interventions (in particular, current treatment practice without the innovation). It is important to include all relevant resources and their valuation in the analysis.

The SHI pricing procedure currently completely refrains from offsetting cost savings elsewhere in the healthcare system with additional costs of another (digital) health solution. In any case, it is important to include all relevant costs from the decision-maker's point of view, which is also recommended by IQWiG.

Although there are very differentiated methods of health economic evaluation and cost accounting, an estimate of the saved costs, determined as the difference of clinical events and multiplied by their care costs from the perspective of health insurance funds (i.e. reimbursement rates), can be used as a pragmatic approximation. This cost difference can represent a possible price ceiling for a savings-based value proposition at the level of health insurance funds (e.g. for a new digital care programme). Similarly, comparisons between DRG revenues and actual costs with and without innovation at the level of individual service providers can enable an approximate estimate of possible savings. This can give an indication of how high a possible surcharge could be and whether savings-based pricing could lead to a convincing business case for the entrepreneur.

1.8 Value-Based Reimbursement

From an economic perspective, added value is also the central reference for pricing in the healthcare system, and health economic evaluation is a method for quantifying added value. However, how added value for decisions on health services can be determined in terms of content in accordance with legal framework conditions in Germany is an issue that has not yet been solved by consensus among all relevant experts and interest groups. Whereas with cost measurement at the level of individual service providers and the implementation of simple cost-minimisation analyses from the perspective of health insurance funds, a sub-area of health economic evaluation methodology is very relevant and widespread in the assessment of medical innovations. The methodology of complete health economic evaluations for SHI decision-making and thus associated with launch activities in Germany has so far been more of a theoretical reference model than a practical decision-making aid (which is often different internationally, e.g. with regard to the United Kingdom).

The price of an additional unit of health benefit associated with a new service might also be expressed in its incremental cost-effectiveness ratio (ICER). It is often represented graphically with the help of a cost-benefit diagram (Fig. 3). It has become common practice to plot benefits on the abscissa and costs on the ordinate, so that a higher slope expresses a higher price per additional health gained. However, this is convention and IQWiG suggests plotting benefits on the ordinate and costs on the abscissa, so that a flattening of the curve can be interpreted as decreasing efficiency.

One first distinguishes between four quadrants: A new intervention can have a higher benefit and be more cost-effective compared to a standard treatment S. Then it would dominate the current standard treatment S and should be introduced in any case (south-east quadrant). The opposite case of a less effective and at the same time

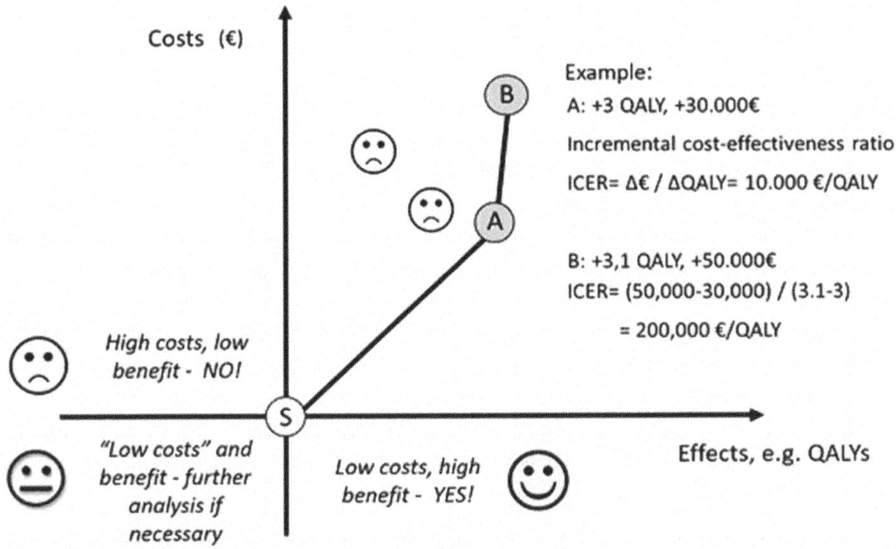

Fig. 3 Cost—benefit quadrants. Source: own representation based on Rogowski (2016, p. 224)

more expensive intervention (North-West quadrant) means that the new intervention is dominated by the standard treatment and should not be adopted. The decision becomes more complex in the two remaining fields, whereby innovations in the South-West quadrant are hardly addressed in the health economic literature. Most innovations that have succeeded in entering the market also fall into the north-east quadrant, i.e. they offer additional benefits at higher costs.

In the first paragraph of this chapter it was said that full economic evaluations in Germany are currently primarily a theoretical reference model (although it should be added that they are central to decision makers such as NICE in the UK). However, this does not limit the usefulness of economic evaluation for structuring a pricing rationale in digital health care, which also applies to Germany.

Decision analytic modelling can provide a quantitative synthesis of the value proposition in healthcare or help to optimize the value proposition (Cf. Briggs et al. 2006). Important elements of decision analytic modelling include:

1. Adequate definition of the relevant goal for the decision-maker (e.g. health measured in QALYs instead of individual customer benefit).
2. Appropriate mapping of the health problem, for which clinical experts are consulted.
3. Correct representation of the structure of the decision problem, which ideally includes the inclusion of all available alternatives—Fig. 3 illustrates that cost-effectiveness is very much dependent on comparator therapies—without an alternative A, the ICER for option B would be €16,129/QALY (€50,000/3.1 QALYs). Thus, all services applicable to the target group should be included or the exclusion of relevant services should at least be well justified.

4. Identification, measurement and evaluation of health outcomes according to the specifications of the decision-makers (this typically includes HTA to incorporate existing clinical studies).
5. Identification, measurement and evaluation of all relevant costs, which strongly depend on the perspective of the decision maker; often a SHI perspective can be taken and costs can be included in the reimbursement amount.
6. Methodologically transparent presentation of results—especially for discussions with the SHI system and use in formal reimbursement processes. The transparent presentation of the method and how a result was calculated is as relevant as the result itself.
7. Appropriate analysis of uncertainty—whereas current health economic methodological standards require so-called probabilistic analyses in which parameter uncertainty is taken into account with model simulations. In the context of the early evaluation, similar to the business plan, it is primarily important to understand the impact of individual parameter changes (such as effectiveness) on the results.

The empirical estimate of a ratio of additional costs and benefits alone does not provide an answer as to whether an innovation offers "added value" at a given price. On the one hand, there are various theoretical answers to this question in the literature. Representatives of the English NICE often argue that there should be a cost-effectiveness threshold that reflects the cost-effectiveness of services that can no longer be financed in view of scarce resources. If the cost-effectiveness is less favourable than this threshold, further benefit is lost from a health system perspective than is generated by the new service, and the price must be reduced or the service excluded from provision. In English decision-making practice, a politically established threshold value range of approximately £20–30,000/QALY is used for this purpose, which is somewhat higher than a currently empirically estimated threshold value of about £13,000/QALY. It should be noted that the empirical estimate is not free of limitations (Cf. Martin et al. 2008) and the (utilitarian) principle of achieving a population-related maximum gain in lifetime and health-related quality of life with the given means is in contradiction to formative legal and ethics principles in Germany. An alternative approach is to estimate an average willingness to pay per QALY in representative surveys, although this is associated with the problem that the estimation results are very heterogeneous and an ubiquitous willingness to pay per QALY can hardly be determined (Cf. Pennington et al. 2015). Finally, IQWiG proposes under the name "efficiency frontier concept" to use the incremental cost-effectiveness of the previously reimbursed service with the greatest health benefit as orientation, which corresponds to the intuition "for 50% more service I am willing to pay 50% more". However, this approach has also been criticized, for example because it attributes a higher value to a certain additional benefit the higher the costs of care in an indication area.

In addition to the extra costs and effects, however measured, other legal, medical and ethics aspects flow into the value judgement as to whether a new health service actually offers "added value" from the point of view of the system. In addition to content-related considerations (e.g. severity of illnesses), procedural requirements (e.g. transparency, participation) also play an important role (Cf. Marckmann 2008).

In German decision-making practice, value-based pricing is currently limited as a formal procedure to new digital health application in the outpatient setting. In this context, a new digital healthcare product is subject to a benefit assessment within the framework with the BfArM (Chapter "Digital Health Applications: DiGAs—Pathway to Reimbursement"). If the BfArM makes a final positive decision on the additional benefit and hence includes the digital health application in the DiGA registry, negotiations on discounts on the list price of the new digital product take place between the DiGA company and the Head association of the statutory health insurance fund (GKV Spitzenverband) based on the benefit assessment (reference). In contrast to the transparent benefit assessment, there are no explicitly predefined criteria for the price negotiation, but rather confidential negotiations. Potentially relevant criteria in the negotiation are the following points according to the framework agreement on price negotiation:

- The BfArM decision on the permanent benefit assessment with the findings made therein, in particular on the additional benefit in relation to the appropriate comparator therapy and the number of patients.
- The benefit assessment of the BfArM to be published on the internet, which forms the basis of the commenting procedure following the publication, and the submitted clinical evidence prepared by the DiGA company.
- The actual selling prices in other European countries (Austria, Belgium, Czech Republic, Denmark, Finland, France, Greece, Ireland, Italy, Netherlands, Portugal, Slovakia, Spain, Sweden, United Kingdom).
- The annual therapy costs of comparable medicinal products suitability is derived from the international standards of evidence-based medicine.

The benefit assessment and information on costs and prices are interpreted by the decision-making body of the GKV Spitzenverband and a decision is made based on this. As of early 2021 there was no negotiation that took place after a BfArM decision. However, it is expected that in addition to the negotiation criteria already mentioned, the severity of the disease as well as the availability of alternatives and the degree of innovation of a new digital solution could also have an influence. Furthermore, the importance of a disease in the public perception (e.g. breast carcinoma) can have an influence on the decision. In addition, political aspects (e.g. innovation promotion/industrial policy) including the political influence of physicians and patient representatives as well as a possible press repercussion can play a role.

In order to optimally plan new digital therapies in the pricing decision environment, companies are recommended to seek contact with decision-makers. These can usually be contacted formally through official consultations or sometimes informally by means of workshops. Furthermore, completed benefit assessments should be evaluated and the current willingness-to-pay and prices of potential comparator therapies relevant for price determination (so-called "price anchors") should be analysed.

1.9 Innovative Pricing Agreements for Digital Health Applications

In order to be able to determine a value-based price, all information regarding the value of the product should be available during the price negotiations between the manufacturer and the head association of statutory health insurance funds (GKV-SV). This is however, not always the case. To some extent the parties involved in the price negotiations need to deal with uncertainties, e.g. with respect to clinical outcomes, epidemiology, and cost impact.

In order to address these uncertainties, innovative pricing agreements could be negotiated to share the risks. The main concepts are summarized in Fig. 4. Based on the uncertainties to be addressed, different innovative pricing arrangements can be delineated. In general, outcomes-based agreements are separated from non-outcomes based agreements (also known as financial-based risk-sharing agreements) (Cf. Urbinati et al. 2017; Carlson et al. 2010; Navarria et al. 2015; Garrison et al. 2013).

Non-outcomes-based agreements can further be separated on population level agreements and patient level agreements. An example for a population level agreement is a price-volume agreement. For this agreement type, the manufacturer allows for price discrimination based on different sales volumes. A utilization cap agreement follows the same mechanism, however is based on patient level (Cf. Garrison et al. 2013).

Outcomes-based agreements link the coverage to clinical outcomes instead of utilization measurements. They can be further separated in Coverage with Evidence Development (CED) and outcomes-based risk-sharing agreements. CED amplify that new medical interventions are only covered for a certain period of time, which

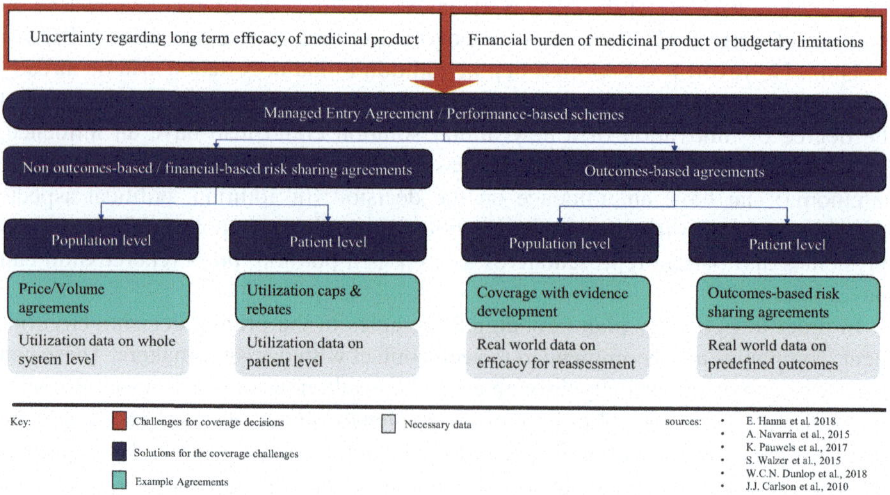

Fig. 4 Excerpt of terminology and concepts on innovative pricing agreements

was agreed on by the payer and manufacturer. During this time, additional data on the long-term effects of the intervention are collected and used for a reassessment of the coverage decision (Cf. Hutton et al. 2007). Outcomes-based risk sharing agreements hold the promise to negotiate truly value based prices. The parties involved in the design of this agreement define outcomes that will be measured once the product is launched to the market. The pricing is directly linked to these outcomes. If a digital health application holds the promise to increase a defined clinical outcome parameter (e.g. overall survival), this parameter could be anchored to an outcomes-based risk-share agreement. Such an approach could primarily be applied to all clinical outcomes that are easily, continuously and consistently measurable. Since some digital health applications are continuously generating data regarding health outcomes of patients, these information could be used as a basis for an innovative price agreement.

Out of the box: Learning from innovative pricing agreements for advanced therapy medicinal products.

A central point of discussion within the field of drug pricing are reimbursement agreements for advanced therapy medicinal products (ATMPs) which include gene therapies, somatic cell therapies and tissue engineered medicinal products (Cf. Jönsson et al. 2019).

Six out of nine ATMPs were granted a non-quantifiable additional benefit by the G-BA. The assessment of Zynteglo® resulted in a hint for a non-quantifiable additional benefit (Cf. Gemeinsamer Bundesausschuss 2020). For Imlygic® no additional benefit could be proven (Cf. Gemeinsamer Bundesausschuss 2016). The potential value of Luxturna® was classified as a hint for a major additional benefit (Cf. Gemeinsamer Bundesausschuss 2019).

The reimbursement decisions for ATMPs with transformative effects incorporate innovative, outcomes-based reimbursement agreements (Cf. Jorgensen et al. 2020). The agreements are negotiated between cooperation of insurances and the marketing authorization holders. For Alofisel®, Yescarta®, Kymriah®, Zynteglo® and Zolgensma® outcomes-based risk-sharing agreements with individual payers have been negotiated (Cf. Walzer et al. 2019). These agreements are based on a full upfront payment by the payer with confidential discounts. The marketing authorization holder partially or fully refunds the payer, if the therapy does not result in the anticipated treatment success (Cf. Jorgensen et al. 2020).

1.10 Strategic Consideration in Digital Healthcare Pricing

A strategic aspect of product positioning—and thus also of price determination—has already become clear from the consideration of the ICER: added value is defined by the comparative intervention. This can be partly influenced by the manufacturer's product strategy: innovative services can often be applied in different indication areas (and thus possibly, for example, in disease areas with or without existing treatment options) or at different points in the treatment pathway (e.g. first, second or third line treatment in the case of a digital health service). In the development process, the company can focus early on a niche in which comparatively higher prices can be achieved. In addition, companies can try to position their services in a high-price niche first and then successively expand the area of application. However, it should be borne in mind that, from the point of view of the SHI, the cost-effectiveness in the patient group in which the cost-effectiveness ratio is the least favourable is basically decisive for pricing (Cf. Claxton et al. 2011).

In response to this, this is also at the same time a strategic opportunity for product positioning for both DiGA companies and the SHI: if another, high-priced intervention or, for example, a low-cost DiGA were used alone as the comparator product in the process of reimbursement decision and price negotiation, significant influence could be exerted on the outcome even before the cost-benefit assessment.

Closely related to this is the expected number of (patient) cases. Even if a therapy is considered cost-effective on the basis of economic evaluation (i.e. its cost-benefit ratio is below a threshold value accepted in a health system), this assumption means an additional expenditure for the budget. Therefore, many countries, e.g. Belgium and Germany, include a budget impact analysis to verify not only the "suitability" of the reimbursement but also the "reasonability" for the system, to refer to the terms mentioned in the SGB V. The more cases and hence the higher the budget impact, the lower, ceteris paribus, the willingness to pay for high prices would be.

Finally, a third aspect of major importance is the orientation of decision-makers to prices in other countries ("external price referencing"). This external price referencing can be applied in different ways. Some countries only accept the lowest price from a defined group of countries as their own price, others take an average from several countries as the price determination and still others use foreign prices informally as a further argument for discounting possible entry prices from the industry. As a consequence, this leads companies to strategically market entry planning in different health systems to bring about a price-maximising "launch sequencing"—strategically determined sequence of the introduction of new digital products.

References

Briggs, A., Claxton, K., Sculpher, M. (2006): Decision modelling for health economic evaluation, Oxford u. a., Oxford Univ. Press.

Carlson, J.J., Sullivan, S.D., Garrison, L.P., Neumann, P.J., Veenstra, D.L. (2010): Linking payment to health outcomes: a taxonomy and examination of performance-based reimbursement schemes between healthcare payers and manufacturers. Health Policy; 96(3):179–90.

Claxton, K., Sculpher, M., Carroll, S. (2011): Value-based pricing for pharmaceuticals: Its role, specification and prospects in a newly devolved NHS. CHE Research Paper. York, UK, University of York.

Drummond, M. F. (2005): Methods for the economic evaluation of health care programmes, Oxford, Oxford Univ. Press.

Frodl, A. (2011): Organisation im Gesundheitsbetrieb Betriebswirtschaft für das Gesundheitswesen. Wiesbaden, Gabler Verlag/Springer Fachmedien Wiesbaden GmbH.

Garrison, Jr. L.P., Towse, A., Briggs, A., de Pouvourville, G., Grueger, J., Mohr, P.E., et al. (2013): Performancebased risk-sharing arrangements—good practices for design, implementation, and evaluation: report of the ISPOR good practices for performance-based risk-sharing arrangements task force. Value in Health 16(5):703–19.

Gemeinsamer Bundesausschuss. (2016): Talimogen laherparepvec BAnz AT 30.12.2016 B42016 [Available from: https://www.g-ba.de/beschluesse/2203/].

Gemeinsamer Bundesausschuss. (2019): Beschluss des Gemeinsamen Bun-desausschusses über eine Änderung der Arzneimittel-Richtlinie (AM-RL): Anlage XII – Nutzenbewertung von Arzneimitteln mit neuen Wirkstoffen nach § 35a SGB V Voretigen Neparvovec BAnz AT 11.11.2019 B72019 [Available from: https://www.gba.de/beschluesse/3984/].

Gemeinsamer Bundesausschuss. (2020): Beschluss des Gemeinsamen Bun-desausschusses über eine Änderung der Arzneimittel-Richtlinie (AM-RL): Anlage XII – Nutzenbewertung von Arzneimitteln mit neuen Wirkstoffen nach § 35a SGB V Betibeglogene autotemcel (β-Thalassämie) BAnz AT 23.06.2020 B52020 [Available from: https://www.g-ba.de/beschluesse/4291/.

Gregson, N., Sparrowhawk, K., Mauskopf, J., Paul, J. (2005): Pricing medicines: theory and practice, challenges and opportunities. Nat Rev Drug Discov, 4, 121–30.

Hutton, J., Trueman, P., Henshall, C. (2007): Coverage with evidence develop-ment: an examination of conceptual and policy issues. International Journal of Technology Assessment in Health Care 23(4):425–32.

Jorgensen, J., Hanna, E., Kefalas, P. (2020): Outcomes-based reimbursement for gene therapies in practice: the experience of recently launched CAR-T cell therapies in major European countries. J Mark Access Health Policy 8(1):1715536.

Jönsson, B., Hampson, G., Michaels, J., Towse, A., von der Schulenburg, J.-M.G., Wong, O. (2019): Advanced therapy medicinal products and health tech-nology assessment principles and practices for value-based and sustainable healthcare. The European Journal of Health Economics 20(3):427–38.

Keun, F., Prott, R. (2009): Einführung in die Krankenhaus-Kostenrechnung Anpassung an neue Rahmenbedingungen. 7., überarbeitete Auflage ed. Wiesbaden, Gabler Verlag/GWV Fachverlage GmbH.

Krauth, C., Hessel, F., Hansmeier, T., Wasem, J., Seitz, R., Schweikert, B. (2005): Empirische Bewertungssätze in der gesundheitsökonomischen Evaluation: Ein Vorschlag der AG GesundheitsökonomischeMethoden (AG MEG). Gesundheitswesen, 67, 736–46.

Marckmann, G. (2008): Gesundheit und Gerechtigkeit. Bundesgesundheitsblatt Gesundheitsforschung Gesundheitsschutz, 51, 887–94.

Martin, S., Rice, N., Smith, P. C. (2008): Does health care spending improve health outcomes? Evidence from English programme budgeting data. J Health Econ, 27, 826–42.

Navarria, A., Drago, V., Gozzo, L., Longo, L., Mansueto, S., Pignataro, G., et al. (2015) Do the current performance-based schemes in Italy really work? "Success fee": a novel measure for cost-containment of drug expenditure. Value in Health 18(1):131–6.

Pennington, M., Baker, R., Brouwer, W., Mason, H., Hansen, D. G., Robinson, A., Donaldson, C. (2015): Comparing WTP values of different types of QALY gain elicited from the general public. Health Econ, 24, 280–93.

Rogowski, W. (2016): Business Planning Im Gesundheitswesen. Springer Fachmedien Wiesbaden.

Urbinati, D., Rova, A., Mantuano, M. (2017): The Impact of Managed Entry Agreements on Drug Time to Market in Italy. Value in Health 20(9):A703.

Walzer S et al. (2016) Vergütungshöhe und Preissetzung in Wolf Rogowski. Business Planning im Gesundheitswesen. Die Bewertung neuer Gesundheitsleistungen aus unternehmerischer Perspektive. Springer Verlag

Walzer, S., Prada, M., Berard, I., Benazet, F., Greenhill, W., Martinez, D., et al. (2019): Innovative Atmps: Market Access and Reimbursement Decisions in the Eu5: Availability or Not, That Is the Question. Value in Health 22 (Supplement 3):S424.

Telemedicine in Japan: Challenges and Opportunities

Sven Demiya-Dillenburger, Masaaki Isshiki, and Jörg Mahlich

As digitalization of the healthcare system has also gained momentum during the COVID-19 pandemic in Japan, we would like to introduce the status quo of telemedicine and discuss future challenges. The focus lies on online medical consultations by physicians, clinics and hospitals in Japan. During the first wave that peaked in April 2020, Japan temporarily eased restrictions on remote medical care, and allowed physicians to conduct first-time visits online or by telephone and to expand the number of illnesses that can be treated remotely.

In general, the Japanese healthcare system has long been highly acclaimed for its performance in terms of delivering the world's longest average life expectancy at relatively low cost (Reich et al. 2011). However, in recent years, Japan has been struggling with rising healthcare costs, mainly due to its 'super ageing' population (Muramatsu and Akiyama 2011). Already 28% of the population is aged 65 years and over and the share of the elderly population is still on the rise (Table 1). Therefore, total health expenditure in Japan is increasing not only in absolute numbers but also in regard to gross domestic product (GDP). Healthcare observers hope that the above-mentioned reforms in regard to telemedicine could also help Japan to improve the efficiency of its healthcare system and to curb the overall healthcare burden (Kaneko and Nakagawa 2020).

The Japanese Telemedicine Society defines telemedicine as "performing medical practice between far off locations using telecommunication technology" (Tofukuji 2013). Hence, we focus on "virtual" physician's office visits either by video conference or traditional phone. We do not consider doctor to doctor consultations which is another dimension of telemedicine (e.g. second opinion) and has been

S. Demiya-Dillenburger · M. Isshiki
IQVIA Solutions Japan K.K., Tokyo, Japan
e-mail: sven.demiya@iqvia.com

J. Mahlich (✉)
DICE, University of Düsseldorf, Düsseldorf, Germany

S. Walzer (ed.), *Digital Healthcare in Germany*, Contributions to Economics,
https://doi.org/10.1007/978-3-030-94025-6_8

Table 1 Share of population over the age of 65 in 2017 and 2050 (OECD projection)

Population aged 65 years and over in % of total population			
	2017	2050	Difference
United States	15.6	22.0	6.4
United Kingdom	18.2	25.3	7.1
France	19.5	25.6	6.2
Germany	21.3	29.5	8.2
Italy	22.4	33.9	11.5
Japan	27.7	37.7	9.9
Korea	13.8	38.1	24.3
OECD36	17.4	27.1	9.7

Source: OECD Health Statistics 2019, OECD Historical Population Data and Projections Database, 2019

studied more intensively than the doctor-patient relationship in Japanese scientific literature (Ito et al. 2017).

1 Governance

In Japan's current medical system, a universal health insurance system was introduced in 1961, and all citizens are covered by public health insurance (Ministry of Health, Labor and Welfare, Homepage about medical insurance system 2020). The insurance system in which the insured person is enrolled differs by employment status and can be divided into two categories: Employees' Health Insurance (*kenkō-hoken*) and National Health Insurance (*kokumin-kenkō-hoken*). The former mainly comprises cooperative health insurance companies (*kumiai hoken*) for health insurance funds of large companies, health insurance for small business employees (*seifu kansho kenko hoken*) and mutual insurance companies for public employees (*kyosai hoken*). The latter insurance system is mainly for the self-employed, farmers, fishermen and pensioners (Ministry of Health, Labor and Welfare, Medical insurance, Tokyo 2020).

For all insurers, co-payments are between 10% and 30%, depending on age and income (Mahlich and Sruamsiri 2019). Co-payments are the same, both for face-to-face office visits as for telemedicine. Moreover, a financial aid system was introduced in Japan to help support patients with so-called intractable diseases (*nanbyou*), a group that represents less than 0.1% of the population. These illnesses are associated with a high risk of disability and require labour-intensive care. As of 2016, there were approximately 306 diseases classified as *nanbyou*. Those diseases have very low co-payment ceilings that often result in marginal co-payment rates approaching zero. Another major feature of the Japanese medical system is that insured persons can freely visit medical institutions including physicians' practices and receive medical services almost without any restrictions. Therefore, many

Japanese patients turn directly to the hospital emergency service for minor medical conditions.

In addition to insurance fees and direct out of pocket expenses, approximately 40% of national medical expenses are funded by taxes to maintain the universal health insurance system at an affordable level (Ministry of Health, Labor and Welfare, Homepage about medical insurance system 2020). Medical fees for medical examination in both hospital and non-hospital settings are determined by the Japanese Ministry of Health, Labour and Welfare (MHLW; Kōsei-rōdō-shō), which also sets and revises prices for drugs and medical devices. The MHLW receives advice from the Central Social Insurance Medical Council (*Chuo Shakai Hoken Iryo Kyogi Kai*) (commonly called *Chuikyo*). The MHLW appoints the 26 Chuikyo members from academia and various interest groups, including the Japan Medical Association and the Japan Pharmaceutical Association, which represents physicians and pharmacists, respectively. Other members represent the labour unions (Rengo) and employers (Keidanren) (Cassel and Mahlich 2020). Under the health insurance system, medical fees are set at a uniform national level without regional differentiation (Ministry of Health, Labor and Welfare 2020). The medical fee point table not only sets prices for specific medical services but also defines the content and scope of insurance benefits.

2 Regulation

Telemedicine was not planned in Japan and it would have violated the Medical Practitioners' Act (Prohibition of Non-Medical Examination and Treatment) (Medical Practitioners' Act, Article 20 1948). In 1997 the MHLW issued a notification that for initial diagnosis and acute illness, patients should be treated in person (Ministry of Health, Labor and Welfare, A notification from a bureau of MHLW 1997). However, Japanese rules can be interpreted flexibly. For example, Japanese law states that drugs should be dispensed by pharmacists. As early as 1949 the US-led Supreme Command of Allied Powers instructed the Ministry of Health to introduce the separation of prescribing and dispensing. However, the Japan Medical Association managed to insert a loophole in this rule, so the law allows physicians to dispense drugs when this is explicitly demanded by their patients (Mahlich 2007).

The same flexibility can be observed in regard to digital health, where telemedicine is allowed as an exception based on a patient's request, if (a) it is difficult to conduct face-to-face medical care in areas such as secluded parties and remote areas, and (b) remote medical care is acceptable for patients with stable medical conditions who can access a communication system and who have a stable medical treatment environment (Japan Medical Association General Policy Research Organization 2020). In 2015 the restriction to (a) and (b) of the notification of 1997 was opened (Nisseikiso Research Institute 2020). Later, in 2018, revision of the medical fee table established a new online medical fee for some recurrent patients with chronic diseases (e.g. diabetes).

In the past, the reimbursement item “re-examination by telephone, etc.” was stipulated by medical fees but is not premised on regular medical management. For an “online medical treatment” in terms of regular medical management a treatment plan was required. However due to the strict conditions for claiming online medical fees the introduction did not proceed well (Central Social Medical Insurance Council (Chuikyo) 2019a). After the ban on online medical care was lifted in 2018 a study conducted from September to December 2018 by the National Federation of Health Insurance Societies (Kenporen) reported only 39 online consultations among 21 million medical consultations (Central Social Medical Insurance Council (Chuikyo) 2019b).

In February 2020, in response to the spread of new coronavirus infections in Japan, the MHLW announced that patients with chronic diseases resulting in regular medical consultations could temporarily switch to remote medical consultations by means of telecommunication. Later in April 2020, the Ministry announced that first-time medical consultation via telephone or online will also be accepted temporarily. In October 2020, three government cabinet ministers announced this practice will continue regardless of the current pandemic (Nikkei Online 2020).

The above discussion has focused on the practice of Patient-to-Doctor interactions. Patient-to-Pharmacist consultation practice has been influenced by the pandemic as well and hence the situation of medicine administration guidance has also been relaxed. In the past, face-to-face medicine administration guidance was required based on the Pharmaceutical Affairs Law, but after discussions at the 2017 Future Investment Conference, the Pharmaceutical Affairs Law was amended in 2019, and online medicine administration guidance was established and scheduled to come into effect in September 2020. Requirements are met if patients had an online medical consultation and a video call with a pharmacist. Due to the pandemic in April audio calls e.g. telephone and patients with face-to-face medical consultation are also allowed online medicine administration guidance. This is limited to the Covid-19 outbreak and hence restricted in time. For difficult cases such as rare disease diagnosis a new medical consultation fee was established for a Doctor to Medical Expert consultation. This allows primary care doctors with advanced IT equipment to contact specialists remotely.

3 Reimbursement of Digital Health Care

Medical fees are classified into three types: medical, dental and dispensing fees. The medical fee is calculated by adding stipulated numbers of points for the individual medical activities provided (so-called “fee-for-service system”). The unit price for one point is 10 yen. In the medical fee revision of April 2020, the re-examination fee for digital health care was 71 points which is equivalent to 710 yen (ca. 5.70 Euro), while the re-examination fee for face-to-face medical care was 73 points (730 yen). Although the difference in reimbursement fees between face-to face and online appointments is only marginal, the combination with other fees results in higher financial incentives for face-to-face medical care. For example, a diabetic patient will be charged a re-examination fee of 71 points (710 yen) plus a disease specific medical treatment management fee of 100 points (1000 yen) when using telecommunication devices resulting in 171 points (1710 yen). In contrast, for a face-to-face medical treatment reimbursed with 73 points (730 yen) the specific disease medical treatment management fee is 225 points (2250 yen). In addition, the doctor is eligible for an outpatient management fee of 52 points (520 yen). Therefore, the total points sum up to 350 or 3500 yen, which is more than twice as much as for the same examination via telemedicine.

Regarding medical apps, reimbursement is also possible. Reimbursement and pricing decisions follow the same path as medical devices or drugs. The basic pricing rule in Japan uses the comparator method where the price of a new drug or device is based on the reimbursement price of a comparator. Premiums of up to 120% are awarded, depending on the level of 'innovation' or 'usefulness' according to clinical evidence. However, such price premiums are an exception and, if granted, seldom rise above 5% (Mahlich et al. 2017). The first and only app to date that obtained reimbursement is a smoke cessation app by the company CureApp that received reimbursement in November 2020 (Cureapp, Inc.). The app is used together with a portable device that measures carbon monoxide concentration in a patient's breath. The data package submitted to apply for insurance reimbursement was based on a comprehensive set of both clinical trials (Masaki et al. 2019; Nomura et al. 2019; Masaki et al. 2020; Kario et al. 2020) and economic cost effectiveness studies (Muto et al. 2019).

4 Telemedicine During Covid-19

As can be seen from Fig. 1, during the first Coronavirus peak the number of medical institutions able to provide medical care using telephones and information and communications equipment increased by almost 50% from April to May 2020 (from 10,812 to 15,226 out of 110,898 facilities). The latest numbers from October 2020 show that the share of facilities registered for telemedicine services is 15%.

On the other hand, as reported in Fig. 2, most facilities offering telemedicine have only a very low number of actual online appointments. Although this survey by the Japanese MHLW is based on only seven facilities, most (57.1%) responded that there is no demand at all, while the remaining share (42.9%) served less than six patients a month.

A more representative claims data analysis by IQVIA supports this view (Fig. 3) showing that the number of patients receiving telemedicine related services is still low. In August 2020 for example, among 729,311 patients with a medical claim, only 5525 (0.75%) were treated via telemedicine (online or by telephone). On the other hand, this share was only 0.15% 1 year before. The data also reveal that the

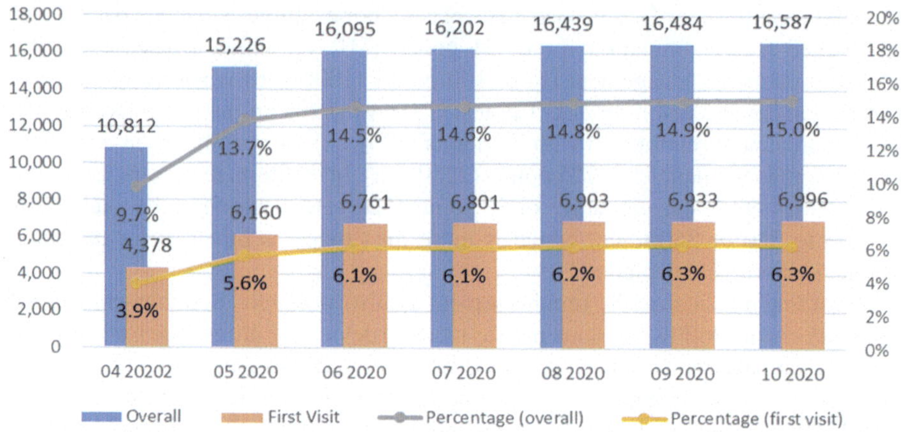

Fig. 1 Changes in the number of medical institutions registered as being able to provide medical care using telephones and information and communications equipment, and the number of medical institutions registered as being able to provide medical care from the first visit. *The denominators for the respective percentages are the sum of hospitals and general clinics used in the Dynamic Survey of Medical Institutions (approximate figures as of the end of April 2020) (110,898 facilities). Source: Japanese Ministry of Health Labour and Welfare 2020, https://www.mhlw.go.jp/content/10803000/000690548.pdf

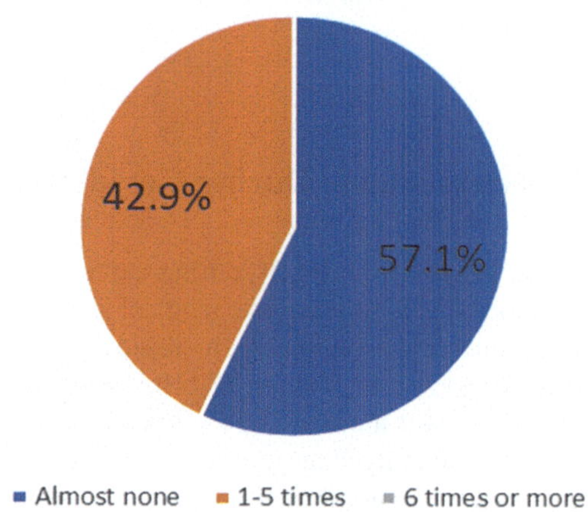

Fig. 2 Monthly average number of online practices by medical institutions providing online practices (N = 7 institutions). Source: Japanese Ministry of Health, Labour, and Welfare, available at: https://www.mhlw.go.jp/content/10803000/000657038.pdf

number of consultations using the telephone exceeded the originally envisioned online consultation system using a PC or smartphone. What is also evident from Fig. 2 is that COVID-19 caused a general fall in office visits to the physician. This trend was also observed in other countries such as Germany (Deutsches Ärzteblatt 2020).

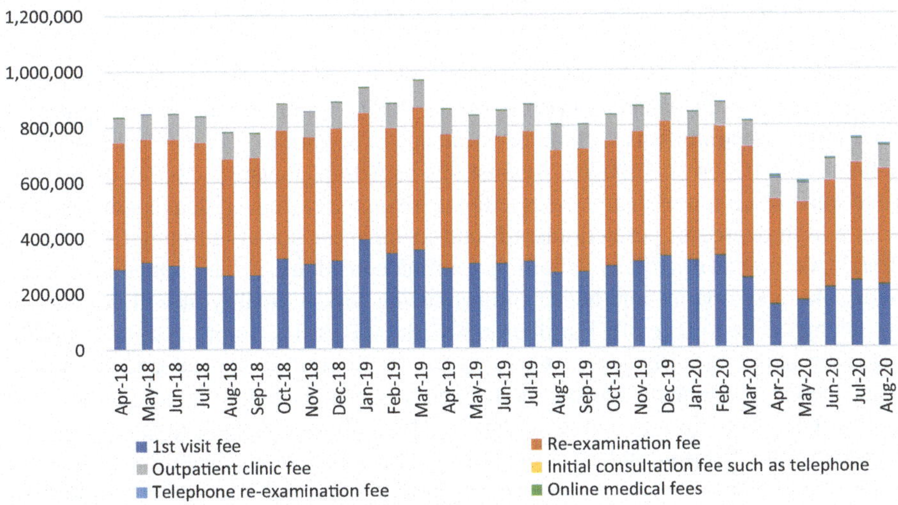

Fig. 3 Number of patients receiving conventional medicine and telemedicine. Source: IQVIA Claims data (April 2018–August 2020)

5 Future Challenges

According to the results of a survey conducted from April to June 2020 (Ministry of Health, Labor and Welfare 2020), the percentage of the elderly aged 61 or over was only about 12.5% of the total in telephone medical services and only 5.5% in online medical services. Therefore, use of telemedicine by the elderly with many chronic diseases will be a challenge. The usability of telemedicine applications is the main influencing factor for user acceptance (Narasimha et al. 2017); and authors emphasize the importance to support the older generation to become familiar with modern technologies. This support could for instance be provided by nurses (van Houwelingen et al. 2016).

Another issue apart from the technological readiness is that the elderly population might also enjoy the social aspect of a doctor's face to face appointment. The desire to chat in the waiting room with peers is an important driver of the number of physician's office visits not only in Japan (Hafner and Mahlich 2016). A recent patient preference study of Japanese Psoriasis patients for instance reported that most respondents prefer to have their treatment administered in a clinic rather than at home (Bolt et al. 2019). This is the opposite of findings of a German study (Schaarschmidt et al. 2011), which found that psoriasis patients considered treatment location at home as the most important attribute for selecting psoriasis treatments. In Japan, a large proportion of people aged over 50 feel lonely (van den Broek 2017), particularly when compared with Western countries (Nicolaisen and Thorsen 2014). Visiting a physician's office might be a strategy to handle loneliness. In line with this reasoning is the fact that Japan (and Korea) have by far the highest numbers of doctor's office consultations among OECD countries (OECD 2018) despite the relatively high co-payments.

Previous research also highlighted the need to understand physicians' perceptions and attitudes toward telehealth (Broens et al. 2007). Determinants of willingness to offer online appointments include performance expectations, i.e. the desire to serve patients well (Chen et al. 2020). Against this backdrop, Japanese doctors might also have some reservations against telemedicine given the extreme risk aversion coupled with a high degree of perfectionism found in Japanese society at large (Synodinos 2001). As long as doctors are afraid that online consultations bear potential risks of overlooking symptoms and hence compromising service quality, it will be difficult for telemedicine to take off. For that reason, there is still a major need for scientific evidence about the efficacy of telemedicine, both from a clinical and economic perspective. A literature review performed in 2016 found only 17 studies that assessed telemedicine outcomes in Japan. The authors conclude that, overall, the scarcity of the literature indicates the need for further rigorous economic evaluation studies of telemedicine programmes in Japan (Akiyama and Yoo 2016). While most studies found moderate savings due to a reduction in transportation costs of several hundred USD (Akematsu and Tsuji 2012; Akematsu et al. 2013), potential downsizes in the quality dimension of medical care are hard to evaluate, which makes cost benefit assessments difficult. Against the backdrop of an aging society with increased cost pressure on the public healthcare budget, economic aspects will certainly become increasingly important. In other areas of the healthcare system, the Japanese government has already applied strong regulation. Regarding prices for drugs and medical devices (including apps), the Japanese government introduced the health technology assessment (HTA) in April 2019, with the clear political aim of achieving better control over prices. Suppliers of drugs and medical devices including medical apps are now required to not only demonstrate that their treatments are clinically effective but also cost-effective and economical. The new legislation mandates that the new treatment should not exceed five million JPY per quality adjusted life-year (QALY) gained (Hasegawa et al. 2020), although there are also ongoing discussions about whether the QALY concept can be transferred to different cultural environments (Mahlich et al. 2018).

Finally, the current situation of telemedicine still heavily relies on traditional interactions between doctors and patients, often still by traditional telecommunication devices. In future this needs to be complemented with remote data collection and digital applications. The above-mentioned smoke cessation app is a vivid example. In this respect, Germany is a good example to look at as it was the first country in the world to reimburse digital health applications (Gerke et al. 2020). Germany requires evidence of a health benefit for reimbursement and it is expected that those evaluation studies will create useful real-world data on the benefits of digital tools for remote patient care (Stern et al. 2020).

6 Conclusion

Telemedicine is still at a relatively early stage despite its current boost due to the COVID-19 pandemic. It is yet to be seen whether Japan can catch up with leading countries in telemedicine such as Australia, China and the United States. Potential hurdles for further utilization of telemedicine include technological readiness mainly by elderly patients and acceptance by risk averse physicians. To increase the incentive for utilization of telemedicine by physicians, it is important not only to advocate the increase in medical care fees but also to enhance the scientific evidence of the efficacy of online medical care. To conclude, an integrative approach is warranted that includes mobile application, remote data collection and analytics.

References

Akematsu Y, Tsuji M. Measuring the effect of telecare on medical expenditures without bias using the propensity score matching method. *Telemed J E Health* 2012;18(10):743-747.

Akematsu Y, Nitta S, Morita K, Tsuji M. Empirical analysis of the long-term effects of telecare use in Nishi-aizu Town, Fukushima Prefecture, Japan. *Technol Health Care* 2013;21(2):173-182.

Akiyama M, Yoo BK. A Systematic Review of the Economic Evaluation of Telemedicine in Japan. *J Prev Med Public Health*. 2016;49(4):183-96.

Bolt T, Kobayashi H, Mahlich J. Patient and Physician Preferences for Therapy Characteristics for Psoriasis: A Discrete Choice Experiment in Japan. *PharmacoEconomics Open* 2019;3, 255–264.

Broens T, Huis in't Veld R, Vollenbroek-Hutten M, Hermens H, van Halteren A, Nieuwenhuis L. Determinants of successful telemedicine implementations: A literature study. *J Telemed Telecare*. 2007;13:303–309.

Cassel D, Mahlich J. What shapes the pharmaceutical market in Japan? Institutional Framework and Challenges of the Japanese Drug Industry, in: Storz C, Taube M (Eds.): *Firms, Institutions, and the State in East Asia,* Marburg: Metropolis, 2020: 137-151.

Central Social Medical Insurance Council (Chuikyo), The 422nd session, [in Japanese], Tokyo 2019a, available: https://www.mhlw.go.jp/content/12404000/000638093.pdf

Central Social Medical Insurance Council (Chuikyo), The 416th session, [in Japanese], Tokyo 2019b, available: https://www.mhlw.go.jp/stf/shingi2/0000205879_00062.html

Chen J, Lan Y-C, Chang Y-W, Chang P-Y. Exploring doctors' willingness to provide online counseling services: The roles of motivations and costs. *Int J Environ Res Public Health*. 2020;17:110.

Cureapp, Inc. (n.d.) https://cureapp-en.blogspot.com/2020/12/cureapp-sc-digital-therapeutic-for.html

Deutsches Ärzteblatt. Arztbesuche: Fallzahlen in Bayerns Praxen zurückgegangen, May 19th, 2020, available: https://www.aerzteblatt.de/nachrichten/113010/Arztbesuche-Fallzahlen-in-Bayerns-Praxen-zurueckgegangen

Gerke S, Stern A, Minssen T. Germany's digital health reforms in the COVID-19 era: lessons and opportunities for other countries. *npj Digit Med* 2020;3:94.

Hafner P, Mahlich J. Determinants of physician's office visits and potential effects of co-payments: evidence from Austria. *Int J Health Plann Manage* 2016;31(3):e192–e203.

Hasegawa M, Komoto S, Shiroiwa T, Fukuda T. Formal Implementation of Cost-Effectiveness Evaluations in Japan: A Unique Health Technology Assessment System. *Value Health* 2020;23 (1), 43–51.

Ito J, Edirippulige S, Aono T, Armfield NR. The use of telemedicine for delivering healthcare in Japan: Systematic review of literature published in Japanese and English languages. *J Telemed Telecare* 2017;23(10):828-834

Japan Medical Association General Policy Research Organization. Current status of online medical care [in Japanese], Tokyo 2020, available: https://www.jmari.med.or.jp/download/RE080.pdf

Kaneko K, Nakagawa I. With apps and remote medicine, Japan offers glimpse of doctor visits in post-corona era, London: Reuters 2020, available: https://www.reuters.com/article/us-health-coronavirus-japan-telehealth-idUSKBN24A01K

Kario K, Nomura A, Harada N, Tanigawa T, So R, Nakagawa K, Suzuki S, Okura A, Hida E, Satake K. A multicenter clinical trial to assess the efficacy of the digital therapeutics for essential hypertension: Rationale and design of the HERB-DH1 trial. *J Clin Hypertens* 2020;22: 1713-1722.

Mahlich J. Die japanische Pharmaindustrie, in: Moerke, A., Walke, A. (eds.), *Japans Zukunftsindustrien*, Heidelberg: Springer 2007, 103-123.

Mahlich J, Sruamsiri R. Co-insurance and health care utilization in Japanese patients with rheumatoid arthritis: a discontinuity regression approach. *Int J Equity Health* 2019;18:13.

Mahlich J, Kamae I, Rossi B. A new Health Technology Assessment System for Japan? Simulating the Potential Impact on the Price of Simeprevir. *Int J Technol Assess Health Care* 2017;33 (1):121-127.

Mahlich J, Dilokthornsakul P, Sruamsiri R, Chaiyakunapruk N. Cultural beliefs, utility values, and health technology assessment. *Cost Eff Resour Alloc* 2018,16, 19.

Masaki K, Tateno H, Kameyama N, Morino E, Watanabe R, Sekine K, Ono T, Satake K, Suzuki S, Nomura A, Betsuyaku T, Fukunaga K. Impact of a Novel Smartphone App (CureApp Smoking Cessation) on Nicotine Dependence: Prospective Single-Arm Interventional Pilot Study. *JMIR Mhealth Uhealth* 2019;7(2):e12694.

Masaki K, Tateno H, Nomura A, Muto T, Suzuki S, Satake K, Hida E, Fukunaga K. A randomized controlled trial of a smoking cessation smartphone application with a carbon monoxide checker. *npj Digit Med* 2020;3(1):35.

Medical Practitioners' Act, Article 20 [in Japanese], Tokyo 1948

Ministry of Health, Labor and Welfare, The 10th Study Group on Review of Guidelines for Proper Implementation of Online Medical Care [in Japanese], Tokyo 2020, available: https://www.mhlw.go.jp/stf/newpage_12769.html

Ministry of Health, Labor and Welfare, A notification from a bureau of MHLW [in Japanese], Tokyo 1997, available: https://www.mhlw.go.jp/bunya/iryou/johoka/dl/h23.pdf

Ministry of Health, Labor and Welfare, Homepage about medical insurance system [in Japanese], Tokyo 2020, available: https://www.mhlw.go.jp/stf/seisakunitsuite/bunya/kenkou_iryou/iryouhoken/iryouhoken01/index.html

Ministry of Health, Labor and Welfare, Medical insurance, Tokyo 2020, available: https://www.mhlw.go.jp/bunya/iryouhoken/iryouhoken01/dl/01_eng.pdf

Muramatsu N, Akiyama H. Japan: Super-Aging Society Preparing for the Future. *Gerontologist* 2011;51(4): 425–432.

Muto T, Tanigawa T, Nomura A, Ogawa T, Ikeda S, Satake K. Cost-Effectiveness Analysis of Digital Therapy for the Patients with Nicotine Dependence. *Japanese Journal of Telemedicine and Telecare* 2019;15 (1):

Narasimha S, Madathil KC, Agnisarman S, et al. Designing telemedicine systems for geriatric patients: a review of the usability studies. *Telemed J E Health* 2017; 23: 459–472

Nicolaisen M, Thorsen K. Who are lonely? Loneliness in different age groups (18–81 years old), using two measures of loneliness. *Int J Aging Hum Dev.* 2014;78:229–57.

Nikkei Online [in Japanese]. Tokyo 2020, available: https://www.nikkei.com/article/DGXMZO64830130Z01C20A0EA3000

Nisseikiso Research Institute. Re-questioning the debate over online medical care-a perspective that is not bound by the pros and cons of the first-time face-to-face principle, Tokyo 2020, available: https://www.nli-research.co.jp/report/detail/id=64672&pno=2?site=nli

Nomura A, Tanigawa T, Muto T, Oga T, Fukushima Y, Kiyosue A, Miyazaki M, Hida E, Satake K. Clinical Efficacy of Telemedicine Compared to Face-to-Face Clinic Visits for Smoking Cessation: Multicenter Open-Label Randomized Controlled Noninferiority Trial. *J Med Internet Res* 2019;21(4):e13520.

OECD 2018. Doctors' consultations (indicator). https://doi.org/10.1787/173dcf26-en.

Reich M, Ikegami N, Shibuya K, Takemi K. 50 years of pursuing a healthy society in Japan. *Lancet* 2011;378(9796):1051-1053.

Schaarschmidt ML, Schmieder A, Umar N, et al. Patient preferences for psoriasis treatments: process characteristics can outweigh outcome attributes. *Arch Dermatol.* 2011;147(11): 1285–94

Stern A, Matthies H, Hagen J, Brönneke J, Debatin J. Want to See the Future of Digital Health Tools? Look to Germany. *Harv Bus Rev* 2020, December 2.

Synodinos N. Understanding Japanese consumers: some important underlying factors. *Jpn Psychol Res.* 2001;43(4):235–48.

Tofukuji T. Definition and Typing of Telemedicine - What is telemedicine? In: Japan Telemedicine and Telecare Association (Ed.): *Telemedicine in Japan.* Tokyo, 2013, available: http://jtta.umin.jp/pdf/telemedicine/telemedicine_in_japan_20131015-2_en.pdf

van den Broek T. Gender differences in the correlates of loneliness among Japanese persons aged 50–70. *Australas J Aging.* 2017;36(3):234–7.

van Houwelingen CT, Moerman AH, Ettema RG, Kort HS, Ten Cate O. Competencies required for nursing telehealth activities: a Delphi-study. *Nurse Educ Today* 2016;39:50-6

Barriers and Opportunities for Digital Therapeutics in the United States

Karen Sandman and Anna Forsythe

Many North American companies and innovators are engaged in development of apps, websites, and platforms to support patients, caregivers, and providers. These technologies have the potential to increase efficiency, improve outcomes, and expand access to care while reducing costs. Another factor driving interest in DTx is the Affordable Care Act and other healthcare reforms, which have shifted the emphasis towards value in care delivery, providing an incentive to deliver cost-effective prevention and management of chronic diseases, which DTx can support (Kvedar et al. 2016). Nonetheless, DTx have not yet had a notable impact on patient care or service delivery in the US. This chapter reviews the status of patient access to DTx in the US with a focus on opportunities for developers to collaborate with payers and other stakeholders to increase the uptake and profitability of potentially beneficial technologies.

A common concern of clinicians, patients, regulators, and payers is how to judge whether the effectiveness of a DTx merits the time, effort, and costs of utilizing the technology. For clinicians, key questions include how to identify effective DTx, support patients in accessing DTx, and use DTx data without undue burden on staff (AMCP Forum 2020). For patients, who typically incur at least some out of pocket costs for DTx, common concerns are whether the technology will improve their health, how much it may cost, data privacy—ease of sharing with approved contacts while protecting private information from others—and how complicated it may be to obtain coverage (AMCP Forum 2020). Regulators, recognizing that DTx are

K. Sandman (✉)
Purple Squirrel Economics, New York, NY, USA

AESARA Inc., Boston, Massachusetts, USA
e-mail: karen@aesara.com

A. Forsythe
Purple Squirrel Economics, New York, NY, USA
e-mail: anna.forsythe@pshta.com

S. Walzer (ed.), *Digital Healthcare in Germany*, Contributions to Economics,
https://doi.org/10.1007/978-3-030-94025-6_9

developed rapidly and evolve continually, have questions about how to evaluate efficacy and safety in a timely and appropriate fashion. The concerns of payers tend to mirror those of other stakeholders, with a particular focus on how to obtain meaningful evidence for value in this new treatment modality (AMCP Forum 2020).

1 Regulation of DTx

There is a growing level of interest in providing safe and appropriately regulated access to DTx in the US. Recognizing the role of regulators in assessing the safety and efficacy of DTx, the Food and Drug Administration (FDA) has approved prescription DTx for several chronic conditions, including asthma (several Digihaler® products from Teva), substance use disorder (reSET® and reSET-O® from Pear Therapeutics), insomnia (Somryst™ from Pear Therapeutics), psychiatric disorders (Abilify Mycite® from Proteus Digital Health), attention deficit hyperactivity disorder (EndeavorRx™ from Akili), and diabetes (iSage^{RX} from Amalgam).

The two main pathways to regulatory approval for DTx are the 510(k) pathway, typically used for medical devices, or the more traditional New Drug Application pathway used for pharmaceuticals (AMCP Forum 2020). Most of the currently approved DTx have been approved via the 510(k) pathway, including reSET-O® and Somryst™. EndeavorRx™ was approved via the de novo premarket review pathway, which is used for low- to moderate-risk devices of a new type; subsequent DTx that are similar to EndeavorRx would be approved via the 510(k) pathway. Abilify Mycite®, which is ingested as part of the drug delivery system, was approved via the pharmaceutical NDA pathway.

It is not always clear if or how a DTx in development needs to be cleared through the FDA, as technologies and regulations are rapidly evolving. The Federal Trade Commission has therefore established an interactive tool to aid companies in determining what federal laws apply to their technologies and in remaining compliant throughout the development and testing process (Federal Trade Commission 2016). The FDA Center for Devices and Radiological Health (CDRH) notes that DTx provide opportunities to empower consumers in healthcare decision-making and self-management as a complement to traditional healthcare settings, with the potential to improve efficiency and quality, increase access, reduce costs, and enhance the personalization of medicine (Center for Devices and Radiological Health 2020). In 2020, CDRH established the Digital Health Center of Excellence, which aims to increase collaboration and provide innovative regulatory approaches to promote efficient development and access to DTx.

2 Sources of Revenue for DTx Developers

In addition to achieving regulatory approval, securing reimbursement and sustainable sources of revenue remains a major hurdle for DTx companies in the US market. Payment for DTx could come from patients themselves, ie, direct-to consumer marketing; employers, who may offer DTx as a benefit; hospitals and other healthcare systems that may provide DTx to their patients; pharmaceutical companies, which may provide DTx access as a means to obtain real-world patient data; or from more traditional US health insurance routes, where DTx may be covered as a pharmacy or medical benefit or via a novel digital benefit pathway (CBPartners 2020).

An important consideration regarding coverage of DTx is that many of the currently available DTx are developed to support the management of chronic diseases, which provides both an opportunity to improve long-term outcomes and a coverage challenge. In a survey by ICON, US payers considered DTx to have high value in improving chronic disease outcomes, particularly by providing monitoring with coaching and immediate feedback to reduce costly exacerbations (ICONplc.com 2020). Historically, US payers have followed a model in which reimbursement is for healthcare encounters and treatments administered, while the costs of prevention and holistic management of chronic disease have largely fallen on the patient (Kvedar et al. 2016). This is in part because of the short-term nature of US health plans: with many Americans switching health plans several times per decade, a managed care payer has limited financial incentive to cover a treatment with long-term cost effectiveness unless there is also clear evidence for short-term cost offsets.

Moreover, some of the current approaches to paying for DTx, such as self-pay and employer coverage for chronic disease management, are unlikely to be adopted for indications where there is not likely to be an immediate cost offset, such as in stroke recovery (Kvedar et al. 2016).

2.1 Direct-to-Consumer Marketing

DTx are unique among medical interventions in that they are frequently marketed directly to the patient as a consumer (Cohen et al. 2020). From 2011 to 2019 in the US, about 21% of DTx companies marketed directly to consumers or planned to do so (Cohen et al. 2020). This approach can address some unmet needs by putting the patient in direct control of their healthcare, bypassing gatekeepers or intermediaries. This can be valuable for patients who have face barriers to care for financial, social, cultural, or geographic reasons. On the other hand, a direct-to-consumer approach is typically less regulated than a prescription therapeutic, and products could be of low value or potentially harmful (Cohen et al. 2020). Products may be making claims that are not properly evaluated, and they may lack appropriate warnings (e.g., fitness products that claim cardiovascular benefits but do not specify which types of cardiac patients should avoid use.)

It is likely that, as DTx evolve, there will be more specific regulations around labeling, similar to existing rules about over-the-counter medications and supplements (Cohen et al. 2020). The expectations are likely to evolve such that well-designed studies would support claims of product value, enabling clinicians to advise patients on DTx products and providing consumers the tools to assess the value of a non-prescription product.

2.2 *Employer Sponsorship*

US employers typically incur significant healthcare costs for their employees, and those companies that have a self-insured plan, where the employer contracts with an insurance company to manage a healthcare plan but covers all costs directly, have a particular interest in containing the costs of prevalent and chronic diseases. Thus, employers may find value in supporting DTx, with their emphasis on prevention and long-term health-promoting behaviors (Kvedar et al. 2016). Several DTx companies therefore have focused on marketing directly to employers, particularly for interventions on prevalent issues such as obesity, inactivity, and smoking (Kvedar et al. 2016). Companies might provide such benefits as part of an employee wellness program, distinct from the health insurance benefit.

Wellness programs might include DTx for insomnia or mental health, even in cases where the employer does not provide health coverage. About 90% of insomnia-related costs, including absenteeism, reduced productivity, and increased risk of accidents, are estimated to be borne by employers (Wickwire 2016). Similarly, depression and anxiety can have a major impact on employee attendance, productivity, and retention, with some estimates finding that depression costs employers over 1 month of employee time per year (Kaiser 2020). There is thus an opportunity for developers to demonstrate the economic return on investment, from the employer perspective, of covering DTx for insomnia and mental health.

A CBPartners survey of US payers in May 2020 found that payers considered employer coverage to be a viable approach to promoting access to DTx (CBPartners 2020). There is currently very little published evidence demonstrating economic benefits of DTx from the employer perspective. Nonetheless, employers generally follow the advice of clinical experts in making decisions regarding DTx coverage, and prioritize health, costs, and employee quality of life (AMCP Forum 2020). Employers may be interested in evidence on patient engagement and adherence with the DTx, and they may consider entering into risk-sharing or value-based agreements with DTx developers (AMCP Forum 2020). Another opportunity for employers to support staff in accessing DTx is to make these products eligible for claims on Healthcare Spending Accounts/Flexible Spending Accounts, which are programs by which employees can spend pre-tax income on out-of-pocket healthcare costs (AMCP Forum 2020).

2.3 Hospital and Healthcare System Coverage

A potential route to funding DTx is for a hospital or healthcare system to cover the costs of providing the therapy to its members at low or no cost. For this to be a viable approach, institutions would need clear evidence of improved outcomes, reduced costs, or higher quality ratings based on offering the DTx. Towards this end, various developers have partnered with hospitals and other healthcare systems to run pilot programs, during which data are collected to assess outcomes and to understand the user experience from the patient and provider points of view. One example is a pilot program that the developers of the DTx myStrength, a behavioral health self-care app, undertook with the Missouri Coalition for Community Behavioral Healthcare, the Missouri Department of Mental Health, and the Missouri Foundation to pilot the product in 25 community mental health clinics in the state of Missouri (Abhulimen and Hirsch 2018). A key objective of this pilot program was the understand the cost impact and return on investment of the tool.

Ultimately, these pilot programs serve multiple purposes. Developers can use the data from the programs to inform the overall product value proposition for clinicians, payers, and other potential customers. Meanwhile, if the outcomes are favorable, hospitals can use the data to inform their own decisions on long-term coverage of the DTx for their population. At the same time, the pilot programs provide an opportunity to educate clinicians on how to integrate DTx into their practices and to expose patients to new methods of disease self-management.

2.4 Pharmaceutical Partnerships

As an alternative to reimbursement, some DTx developers have formed partnerships with biopharma, receiving funding and support to develop products that complement conventional drug therapies (Licholai 2020). There are opportunities to form innovative partnerships in which data gleaned from DTx can support pharmaceutical innovation; a key issue in these arrangements is data privacy and transparency regarding who can access data (AMCP Forum 2020).

2.5 Health Insurance Coverage

A recent Decision Resources Group survey of 157 US Pharmacy & Therapeutics (P&T) committee members found that 25% currently provide coverage for some digital therapeutics, and an additional 45% are interested in providing coverage (Decision Resources Group 2020). Compared with other US payer types, pharmacy benefit managers (PBMs) are considered to be the furthest along in establishing digital formularies (Bias 2019). Indeed, two major US pharmacy benefit managers (PBMs), CVS Caremark and Express Scripts, added mechanisms for coverage of

DTx in 2019, and some smaller payers have followed suit (Decision Resources Group 2020).

Express Scripts developed the Evernorth Digital Health Formulary, which assesses DTx products based on clinical effectiveness, security/privacy, usability features, and economic value (Express Scripts 2020). The formulary covers a range of therapeutic areas, including women's health, diabetes, cardiovascular health, mental health, and chronic pain (Express Scripts 2020). These selected therapeutic areas are in line with the findings of a recent ICON US payer survey, in which respondents identified behavioral health, diabetes, and cardiovascular health as the most applicable indications for DTx (ICONplc.com 2020).

Despite these notable steps towards coverage, many US payers, including Medicare as discussed in the next section, are considerably less advanced in their uptake of DTx. The ICON US payer survey found that respondents considered their organizations to be only moderately prepared for evaluating DTx, in part due to the rapid evolution of the field and small number of prescription products currently available (ICONplc.com 2020). Similarly, a CBPartners survey in May 2020 found that in general, US payers had not developed formal DTx review processes within their own organizations (CBPartners 2020). The ICON survey participants generally noted that DTx would need to have FDA approval and would need to be prescribed in order to gain formulary access (ICONplc.com 2020).

In general, greater awareness of the overall cost of care is associated with higher levels of interest in DTx: the DRG survey found that respondents representing integrated delivery networks, where budgets cover all medical and pharmaceutical costs for members, were most likely to report coverage for DTx (Decision Resources Group 2020). In contrast, respondents from conventional commercial insurance plans, which have separate budgets for medical and pharmaceutical benefits, reported the lowest coverage rates (Decision Resources Group 2020). Among surveyed physicians, 44% overall expressed interest in prescribing DTx, compared with 52% among physicians who provide input to payers on P&T committees (Decision Resources Group 2020).

It has been proposed that risk-sharing contracts may be an opportunity for DTx to begin to engage with managed care payers.

2.6 Medicare Challenges

Medicare, the health plan for elderly Americans, does not currently cover DTx, due to legislation that defines treatments in such a way that DTx do not fall into any covered category. Thus, federal legislation would need to be changed to enable such coverage (AMCP Forum 2020; Licholai 2020). In late 2020, the Centers for Medicare & Medicaid Services proposed new rules for Medicare Coverage of Innovative Technology MCIT), which would allow for 4 years of coverage of a technology after FDA approval (Centers for Medicare and Medicaid Services 2020). The criteria for MCIT coverage would be that the DTx is "reasonable and necessary," i.e., that is it safe and effective, FDA-approved, and appropriate for Medicare patients, meaning that it is within standard medical practice, relevant to and meeting the patient's medical needs, ordered by qualified providers, and at least as beneficial as existing alternatives. The proposed ruling also allows for coverage of any DTx that is covered by commercial insurance. At the end of 4 years, coverage could be continued or denied, but the expectation is that the developer would use the intervening time to strengthen the evidence base supporting the DTx.

As of December 2020, the public comment period for the MCIT ruling is complete, but the ruling has not been implemented. Given that the elderly Medicare population is largely past working age and thus would not receive DTx as an employer benefit, a mechanism for Medicare coverage of DTx is essential for the viability of certain DTx products. Such coverage would be critical to provide developers an incentive to innovate on DTx for conditions prevalent in the elderly, such as dementia and osteoarthritis.

3 Development of Payer-Relevant Evidence for DTx Value

DTx, with its promise of improved patient self-management, offers payers an option to support products that can improve adherence to treatment plans and potentially translate into long-term outcomes. To support decisions regarding DTx coverage, US payers are interested in evidence on the usability, clinical and comparative effectiveness, patient adherence, safety, budget impact and cost effectiveness, and data security (AMCP Forum 2020). A web-based survey of 70 US payers, including health plans, pharmacy benefit managers, and integrated delivery networks found that payers prioritized certain types of evidence in making decisions regarding DTx: return on investment evaluation (80%), real-world evidence/observational studies (79%), relevance to current care pathways (69%), randomized controlled trials (64%), FDA approval (46%), and disease state classification with tier guidance (41%) (Bias 2019).

Respondents to both the ICON and CBPartners payer surveys noted that DTx ideally should have real-world outcomes evidence provided (CBPartners 2020; ICONplc.com 2020). DTx developers have, therefore, focused on generating health economic evidence to demonstrate long-term outcomes, cost savings, and cost offsets (Licholai 2020).

The CBPartners survey noted that pilot programs to test DTx may be helpful in collecting evidence on cost of care, prolonged patient engagement with the DTx, and the short-term return on investment that US payers need to see, given the frequent turnover of members in a health plan (CBPartners 2020).

3.1 Emerging Evidence for Economic Value of DTx in the US

There is a growing body of evidence on the budget impact and cost effectiveness of DTx in the US. Table 1 reviews economic evaluations of DTx conducted from the

Table 1 Economic evaluations of DTx from the US perspective

Product and indication	Key findings
Livongo for diabetes program, a mobile app that combines blood glucose testing and access to diabetes educators with education and tools (Whaley et al. 2019)	By comparing plan members with diabetes who did or did not enroll in Livongo, the study found reductions in overall medical spending after 1 year on Livongo, with greater reductions for active users of the program Major sources of savings were reductions in spending for diabetes-related and office-based services
reSET-O® for opioid use disorder in patients also receiving treatment with buprenorphine (Wang et al. 2021)	Using claims analysis, 12-week HCRU costs were estimated for patients considered adherent or nonadherent to buprenorphine (without DTx) Clinical trial outcomes were used to estimate differential rate of buprenorphine adherence in patients using reSET-O® Cost effectiveness modeling found an ICER of $18.70/percentage point increase in adherence for addition of reSET-O® Budget impact of reSET-O® over 12 weeks of treatment was 0.003 PMPM
reSET-O® for opioid use disorder in patients also receiving treatment with buprenorphine (Velez et al. 2020)	In this retrospective claims study, HCRU was assessed up to 6 months before and after initiation of reSET-O® Among patients who received reSET-O®, HCRU decreased, with significant ($p < 0.05$) reductions in inpatient stays and clinical encounters for drug testing, psychiatry, and other pathology/laboratory, with a net savings of $2150 per patient over 6 months
Digital diabetes prevention program among a workforce population (Sweet et al. 2020)	In this longitudinal, observational claims analysis of costs and HCRU among 2027 adult participants, at 1 year, all-cause healthcare spending was reduced by $1169 relative to controls who did not participate ($p = 0.01$), with a $699 reduction in inpatient costs ($p = 0.001$) Key drivers of cost savings were reductions in hospital admissions and length of stay In the second year, there was a trend towards reduced costs but the difference was not significant
myStrength digital behavioral health self-care tool among a Missouri Medicaid population (Abhulimen and Hirsch 2018)	In this observational study comparing 799 people who registered for myStrength and 715 matched controls, overall cost reductions were $382 for users over 11 months, in inpatient, emergency, and general and psychiatric outpatient care and outpatient psychotherapy The ROI for the tool was estimated at 142% to 695%

HCRU: healthcare resource utilization; ICER: incremental cost effectiveness ratio; PMPM: per member per month; ROI: return on investment

US perspective. In general, these studies have found cost savings and offsets associated with DTx, although the evidence base informing economic models remains limited.

3.2 ICER Assessment of DTx

While there is no primary health technology assessment (HTA) body in the US, the Institute for Clinical and Economic Review (ICER) has become a leading source of evidence review for therapeutics. In 2020, ICER conducted its first review of DTx, focusing on treatments for opioid use disorder, including reSET-O®, Connections, and DynamiCare (ICER 2020). The final report noted that none of the DTx products had randomized clinical trial data comparing the addition of the digital intervention to medication-assisted treatment alone; the evidence available for each product was not published in a peer-reviewed journal, only reported short-term outcomes, and lacked patient-relevant endpoints such as ER visits or return to work. The only product that could be assessed for cost effectiveness was reSET-O®, which was deemed to be cost-effective only if the short-term benefits are assumed to persist far beyond the timeframe of the clinical trial that was used in the model (ICER 2020).

Noting the risk of putting resources towards technologies that have not been demonstrated effective, considering the seriousness of the opioid epidemic, ICER recommended that developers conduct randomized controlled trials, powered to identify subgroups most likely to benefit from DTx, to strengthen their evidence base. ICER also suggested alternative funding schemes such as outcomes-based contracting and recommended developing a full evidence dossier for DTx (ICER 2020).

4 Future Directions

Across all stakeholders in the US, there is a clear need for rigorous and validated evidence to support DTx. Payers, clinicians, and employers recognize the potential for DTx to provide cost-effective improvements in long-term outcomes, particularly for chronic diseases, but currently, there is scant evidence demonstrating actual clinical and economic value. There are operational barriers to DTx coverage as well, with private payers working to establish whether these products will be covered through existing benefits or a novel pathway, and Medicare unable to cover DTx under existing legislation.

The field of DTx, particularly from the reimbursement and access perspective, is very new. There are opportunities to establish best practices to demonstrate the economic value of DTx and to determine the appropriate funding routes for these innovative technologies. The development of a standardized process for evaluating the value of DTx, similar to the Academy of Managed Care Pharmacy (AMCP) dossier format for biopharmaceuticals, may be a starting point for more consistent assessments across therapeutic areas, payers, and products (AMCP Forum 2020).

References

S. Abhulimen and A. Hirsch, 'Quantifying the economic impact of a digital self-care behavioral health platform on Missouri Medicaid expenditures', *Journal of Medical Economics*, vol. 21, no. 11, pp. 1084–1090, Nov. 2018, doi: https://doi.org/10.1080/13696998.2018.1510834.

AMCP Forum, 'AMCP Partnership Forum: Digital Therapeutics—What Are They and Where Do They Fit in Pharmacy and Medical Benefits?', *JMCP*, vol. 26, no. 5, pp. 674–681, May 2020, doi: https://doi.org/10.18553/jmcp.2020.19418.

S. Bias, 'Assessing Barriers to Inclusion of Digital Therapeutics on Formulary: A Cross-Sectional Study Across Health Plans, PBMs, and IDNs', presented at the AMCP Nexus 2019, Oct. 2019.

CBPartners, 'Access to Digital Therapeutics in a Post-COVID-19 World', *CBPartners*, Jul. 14, 2020. https://www.cbpartners.com/access-to-digital-therapeutics-in-a-post-covid-19-world/ (accessed Dec. 28, 2020).

Center for Devices and Radiological Health, 'What is Digital Health?', *FDA*, Sep. 2020, Accessed: Dec. 27, 2020. [Online]. Available: https://www.fda.gov/medical-devices/digital-health-center-excellence/what-digital-health.

Centers for Medicare & Medicaid Services, 'Medicare Program; Medicare Coverage of Innovative Technology (MCIT) and Definition of "Reasonable and Necessary"', *Federal Register*, Sep. 01, 2020. https://www.federalregister.gov/documents/2020/09/01/2020-19289/medicare-program-medicare-coverage-of-innovative-technology-mcit-and-definition-of-reasonable-and (accessed Dec. 29, 2020).

A. B. Cohen, S. C. Mathews, E. R. Dorsey, D. W. Bates, and K. Safavi, 'Direct-to-consumer digital health', *The Lancet Digital Health*, vol. 2, no. 4, pp. e163–e165, Apr. 2020, doi: https://doi.org/10.1016/S2589-7500(20)30057-1.

Decision Resources Group, 'U.S. payers are warming up to covering digital therapeutics | Downloads', *DRG*, Mar. 31, 2020. https://decisionresourcesgroup.com/downloads/u-s-payers-warming-covering-digital-therapeutics/ (accessed Dec. 23, 2020).

Express Scripts, 'Express Scripts | Digital Health Formulary'. https://my.express-scripts.com/digital-health-formulary.html (accessed Dec. 24, 2020).

Federal Trade Commission, 'Mobile Health Apps Interactive Tool', *Federal Trade Commission*, Apr. 04, 2016. https://www.ftc.gov/tips-advice/business-center/guidance/mobile-health-apps-interactive-tool (accessed Dec. 27, 2020).

ICER, 'Opioid Epidemic: Digital Health Technologies', *ICER*. https://icer.org/assessment/opioids-digital-apps-2020/ (accessed Dec. 29, 2020).

ICONplc.com, 'Payers' Perspectives on Digital Therapeutics: In-Depth Interviews Reveal What Manufacturers Can Expect', 2020.

Kaiser, 'How to pick employee mental health apps | Kaiser Permanente', *Business Health Care | Choose Better | Kaiser Permanente ®*. https://business.kaiserpermanente.org/insights/mental-health-workplace/mental-health-apps-workforce-wellness (accessed Dec. 29, 2020).

J. C. Kvedar, A. L. Fogel, E. Elenko, and D. Zohar, 'Digital medicine's march on chronic disease', *Nat Biotechnol*, vol. 34, no. 3, pp. 239–246, Mar. 2016, doi: https://doi.org/10.1038/nbt.3495.

G. Licholai, 'Digital Therapeutics Leaders Focus On Reimbursement', *Forbes*. https://www.forbes.com/sites/greglicholai/2020/02/23/digital-therapeutics-leaders-focus-on-reimbursement/ (accessed Dec. 23, 2020).

C. C. Sweet, C. B. Jasik, A. Diebold, A. DuPuis, and B. Jendretzke, 'Cost Savings and Reduced Health Care Utilization Associated with Participation in a Digital Diabetes Prevention Program in an Adult Workforce Population', *JHEOR*, vol. 7, no. 2, pp. 139–147, Aug. 2020, doi: https://doi.org/10.36469/jheor.2020.14529.

F. F. Velez, S. Colman, L. Kauffman, C. Ruetsch, and K. Anastassopoulos, 'Real-world reduction in healthcare resource utilization following treatment of opioid use disorder with reSET-O, a novel prescription digital therapeutic', *Expert Review of Pharmacoeconomics & Outcomes Research*, vol. 0, no. 0, pp. 1–8, Nov. 2020, doi: https://doi.org/10.1080/14737167.2021.1840357.

W. Wang, N. G. Lowe, A. Jalali, and S. M. Murphy, 'Economic modeling of reSET-O, a prescription digital therapeutic for patients with opioid use disorder', *Journal of Medical Economics*, vol. 24, no. 1, pp. 61–68, Jan. 2021, doi: https://doi.org/10.1080/13696998.2020.1858581.

C. M. Whaley *et al.*, 'Reduced medical spending associated with increased use of a remote diabetes management program and lower mean blood glucose values', *Journal of Medical Economics*, vol. 22, no. 9, pp. 869–877, Sep. 2019, doi: https://doi.org/10.1080/13696998.2019.1609483.

E. M. Wickwire, 'Value-Based Sleep in the Workplace', *Sleep*, vol. 39, no. 10, pp. 1767–1768, Oct. 2016, doi: https://doi.org/10.5665/sleep.6150.

The manufacturer's authorised representative in the EU is Springer Nature Customer Service Centre GmbH, Europaplatz 3, 69115 Heidelberg, Germany. If you have any concerns regarding our products, please contact ProductSafety@springernature.com

Printed and bound by CPI Group (UK) Ltd, Croydon, CR0 4YY
22/09/2026
02220961-0012